ies

A-level Study Guide

ICT

Martin Barrall

J V Kelso-Mitchell

Revision Express

Acknowledgements

The publishers thank Dave Parry, Education Consultant, for his assistance.

Box shot reprinted with permission from Microsoft Corporation. Screen shots reprinted by permission from Microsoft Corporation. Microsoft, Encarta, MSN, and Windows are either registered trademarks or trademarks of Microsoft Corporation in the United States and/or other countries. *ICT* is an independent publication and is not affiliated with, nor has it been authorised, sponsored, or otherwise approved by Microsoft Corporation.

In some instances we have been unable to trace the owners of copyright material, and we would appreciate any information that would enable us to do so.

Series Consultants: Geoff Black and Stuart Wall

Pearson Education Limited
Edinburgh Gate, Harlow
Essex CM20 2JE, England
and Associated Companies throughout the world
www.pearsoned.co.uk

© Pearson Education Limited 2005

The rights of Martin Barrall and J V Kelso-Mitchell to be identified as authors of this Work has been asserted by them in accordance with the Copyright, Designs and Patents Act 1988.

British Library Cataloguing-in-Publication Data
A catalogue entry for this title is available from the British Library.

ISBN 1-405-82365-8

First published 2005

10 9 8 7 6 5 4 3 2 1
09 08 07 06 05

Set by 35 in Univers, Cheltenham
Printed by Ashford Colour Press, Gosport, Hants

Hardware and software

Hardware and software are equally important in the majority of computer systems. In order to create effective systems, users have many decisions to make regarding elements, from the microprocessor to the operating system, and from specifying the makeup of a bespoke solution to battling with applications generators to satisfy a special purpose. Internal and external components of these systems are usually what define their purpose.

Exam themes

→ The types and capabilities of hardware and software

→ The effect that hardware and software design has on the user

→ The internal components of the microprocessor

→ Input and output devices and their application

→ Purposes of operating systems

→ Adequate and appropriate backup and security

→ The role of communications in ICT and society

→ Language – groupings and translation methods

→ Health and safety issues regarding hardware

Topic checklist

○ AS ● A2

	OCR	EDEXCEL	AQA
Hardware – types and capabilities	○	○	○
Internal components	○	○	
Input and output devices	○	○	○
Software – types and capabilities	○	○	○
Operating systems	○	○	○
General and special purpose systems	○	○●	○
Backup and security		○	○
Role of communications	○●	○	○
Effect of hardware and software on human–computer interface	○		○
Language group hierarchies and translation methods	○	○	○

Hardware – types and capabilities

Consider first the physical configuration of a computer system; different configurations can produce systems with very specific capabilities and purposes.

Personal computers

Originally (early 1980s) intended as standalone machines for personal use, later becoming popular for administrative functions.

The components in most cases were:

→ Base unit, including a limited processor.
→ Monochrome monitor.
→ Basic monochrome printer (probably dot matrix).
→ Keyboard.
→ Secondary storage facility – floppy disk or magnetic tape (no hard disk, sometimes twin floppies).

In the 1970s for the first time, PCs became available to home users and many manufacturers sold large volumes of these simple PCs. Long forgotten names like Sinclair, Commodore and BBC sold very well. They were difficult to use, slow and very low on memory. Some operated through household televisions (which interestingly is exactly what is happening again, with Sky's Open Keyboard and keyboards for digital TVs).

Throughout the mid-1980s, prices decreased and performance improved due to development of components. The standard for personal computing is now the multi-media machine, whose increased list of items is:

→ Base unit, including a very powerful processor.
→ Visual display unit, colour – low emission (could be flat screen).
→ Keyboard and mouse.
→ Colour printer(s) laser or ink jet.
→ Speakers or sound systems.
→ Secondary storage – HDD, FDD, CD writer DVD.
→ Internal modem for Internet link.

Using multi-media machines, along with extra components (e.g., scanners, digital cameras), enables the user to produce work of a high standard without leaving their own home. This started a new wave of home working. Information became highly portable with a knock-on effect for businesses' locations. If need be, work can be transported on a laptop or palm top machine or via telephone lines.

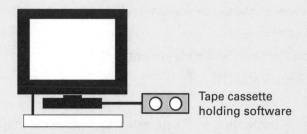

Tape cassette holding software

An early PC keyboard and integrated computer

> *"Refers to objects that you can actually touch, like disks, disk drives, display screens, keyboards, printers, boards, and chips."*
>
> www.pcwebopedia.com

Watch out!

PC refers to computers for personal or individual use – it does not only refer to IBM compatible machines, but all systems for personal use.

Take note

Open keyboards are wire-free keyboards that allow Internet access via the home digital TV provider.

Checkpoint 1

Define the term 'PC'.

The jargon

HDD – Hard Disk Drive.
FDD – Floppy Disk Drive.
DVD – Digital Versatile Disk.

Checkpoint 2

What is the difference between 'standalone' and 'networked' computers?

Check the net

Colossus, the code-breaking computer, broken up after the Second World War and kept secret for 50 years, still forms the basis for all computer languages. Fascinating site at:
www.force9.co.uk/colossus

The integration of computer systems into commerce has revolutionised the way we do business. Systems can be made up of standalone machines but generally consist of networks of computers, all working together to provide efficient services.

→ **EPOS** (electronic point of sale). Enables vendors to process sales and organise stock control systems more effectively through the use of barcodes.
→ **EFTPOS** (electronic funds transfer point of sale). Developed from EPOS, inaugurating the cashless society. With EFTPOS, debits (and credits) can be allocated to current account balances and requests for payment applied to credit card accounts.
→ **E-Commerce**. This technology involves the use of the Internet to 'do business'. It can be used to purchase services or products.

The potential of hardware used in commercial systems is still being explored. Use of modems and the Internet have powered the growth of virtual shopping and electronic commerce. Hardware for commercial systems tends to be more robust than its counterpart in personal computing, and is tailored accordingly. The market for this is dominated by companies such as Dell, IBM, ICL, etc.

Industrial computers ●●●

Hardware in this sector is further specialised. Applications and capabilities range from control in bottling plants to safety equipment in nuclear power stations. Quite often real systems are designed and developed after consideration of possible outcomes derived from simulations and modelling scenarios.

Industrial systems are aimed at situations that:

→ Could be dangerous to humans.
→ Involve boring repetitive tasks.
→ Are low on the list of desirable (though non-dangerous) jobs.
→ Require a level of precision with low tolerance.

Links

See pages 8 and 9 for some of the devices used in commercial systems.

Watch out!

EPOS and EFTPOS are not automatically connected to a stock control system.

Checkpoint 3

State one advantage and one disadvantage of using computers is a commercial environment.

The jargon

Tolerance – the margin of error.

Exam question   answer: page 24

A motor spares shop has electronic tills that can process and store files. This is linked to a server in the office. Special offers and price updates to the tills are made via the server. The owner is the only person allowed to update prices. All sales data is sent to the server.

Discuss the advantages and disadvantages using such as system bearing in mind that the till has its own processor.   (15 min)

Internal components

Some internal components are required to enable the computer to function. Some enhance the computing environment, for example, adding 3D graphics cards will enhance the performance of your monitor and increase your enjoyment when playing educational games!

The microprocessor ●●●

Major components are:

→ **ALU** (arithmetic logic unit). The part of a microprocessor that processes and manipulates data.
→ **Accumulator.** A storage register within the ALU that holds data currently being processed.
→ **Arithmetic register.** A storage register that holds both the results of calculations and the operands used to calculate.
→ **CU** (control unit). Used to manage the operation of the microprocessor, ensuring that data gets from one location to another, as required.
→ **Registers.** Used as temporary storage. Some (accumulator and arithmetic register) are utilised during the 'fetch, decode and execute' cycle. Others are reserved for use by the program being executed:
  Program counter
  Address register
  Memory address register
  Memory buffer register

Busses ●●●

In order for each of the elements of a microprocessor to fulfil their tasks, they need to be supplied with data. This is done via the Bus.

→ Address Bus – manages addresses and indexes.
→ Data Bus – ferries data to and from the ALU.
→ Control Bus – oversees instructions to I/O.

Cards ●●●

Cards are PCBs placed inside a computer's base unit, which create connectivity between the devices. Types are:

→ **Motherboard** or mainboard. Houses the microprocessor and main memory. It is a PCB with space for one or more microprocessor(s), RAM and expansion slots for other cards or items of hardware.
→ **Interface card.** Permits communication with peripherals (hardware, another computer, MIDI) and is plugged into an expansion slot.
→ **Parallel port.** Standard interface card that allows both input and output at high speed. Data is transmitted and received in small groups simultaneously. Also known as a centronics card. Mostly used for printing or game-play.

Watch out!

The microprocessor is the type we associate with multi-media computers. It may be referred to as a CPU, but a CPU generally includes main memory – a microprocessor does not have main memory on board.

Take note

Make definition cards for each of the terms in **bold**.

The jargon

The fetch, decode and execute cycle refers to the actions performed on instructions. They are *fetched* from memory, *decoded* by the ALU and are then run or *executed*.

The jargon

I/O – Input/Output.

The jargon

PCB – Printed Circuit Board.
RAM – Random Access Memory.

Take note

Make notes on the terms highlighted in **bold**.

The jargon

MIDI – Musical Instrument Digital Interface.

→ **Serial port.** Another standard interface card that is also known as RS232. Data is transmitted and received one byte at a time. Data transmission is slower than with a parallel port but is more reliable over distance. One common use is for a mouse or keyboard.

→ **USB port.** The universal serial bus attempts to the solve problems of connecting devices to computers. The ports already supplied had specific hardware that would need to use them so a new form of connection was required.

Memory

Even the simplest tasks, such as sorting two numbers into order of size, cannot be achieved without memory and no permanent records of work could exist without memory.

Main memory

→ **Cache.** Very fast memory utilised for holding frequently used data. It lies between the microprocessor and RAM.

→ **RAM** (random access memory). Memory used as temporary storage. RAM is not pre-filled. RAM becomes occupied by data when the computer is in use. This will be a mixture of data used to operate the computer and data used to run programs.

→ **ROM** (read only memory). Where instructions are permanently etched at manufacture. The contents of ROM cannot be altered. Some basic instructions for booting up of the system will be ROM-based to ensure system access.

Both Cache and RAM are known as volatile forms of memory. When power to the computer is cut off, the content of the memory is lost.

Secondary memory

→ **Floppy** and **hard drives**. Will usually be supplied as part of a multi-media computer and can be used to create permanent records on magnetic media.

→ **Magnetic tape.** Commonly used in commercial and industrial systems to back-up large amounts of data.

→ **DVD** and **CD**. Non-magnetic forms of data storage.

These are non-volatile methods of data storage, i.e. they will retain their contents with or without power.

Exam questions   answers: page 24

Plug and play allows you to insert additional boards into your computer with ease.

(a) Give *two* examples when a systems administrator might want to add an internal board to a system.

(b) What does plug and play mean?

(c) What would a systems administrator have to do if the operating system did not support plug and play. (10 min)

Checkpoint 1

Why do you think that parallel ports are best suited to printing and game-play and likewise, why is serial best for keyboard and mice?

Check the net

An interesting history of computer development can be found at www.internetvalley.com

Checkpoint 2

Why do you think USB ports have been welcomed by both manufacturers and the public?

Example

Some microcomputers use RISC (Reduced Instruction Set Computers) architecture that utilises ROM by etching on more of the operating instructions, enabling faster running.

Links

Pages 16 and 17 have more information on storage devices.

The jargon

Portable memory cards are becoming popular and are very cheap. These small devices plug into the USB port, can be loaded with information and transferred to another PC via its USB port.

Input and output devices

In order to make use of a computer, the user must be able to insert and extract data in as straightforward and appropriate a way as possible.

Manual input ●●●

The following devices are commonly used methods of data input:

→ **Bar code reader.** Uses light to read bar code data and translates this into product information.

→ **Digitiser** – graphics tablet. The use of a pen or stylus is detected by the computer, translated into X–Y co-ordinates and the position held in memory.

→ **Digital camera.** Images produced can be transmitted to a computer and held as bitmaps.

→ **Joystick.** Directions and buttons pressed are detected and the screen output alters accordingly.

→ **Keyboard.** Can be a slow method of data input but sometimes the only option. May lead to transcription errors or repetitive strain injury.

→ **Key pad.** A derivation of the keyboard which uses only numbers.

→ **Light pen.** Contains a sensor which, when used in close proximity to the screen, is detected by the software through the light being blocked. Can be used to 'drag and drop' items if required.

→ **MICR.** Commonly used to encode data that may be open to fraud. Magnetic ink is printed on (for example) a cheque and can be used to help process them quickly.

→ **Mouse.** Used more as a selector of data than as a traditional data input device, although it can be used as such. For example, a section of a graphic can be marked and cut. The user can then paste the contents on the clipboard. In this case, data input can be said to have occurred.

→ **OMR.** A pre-printed form with boxes to be filled with lead or black ink or left empty. Light is then passed over the document and, where it is not reflected, the location is calculated and stored.

→ **Portable devices.** Used to record data as it arises and processed as a batch later.

→ **Scanner/OCR** (optical character recognition). The scanner digitises images or printed text. OCR scans text and can translate in order to manipulate.

→ **Smart card.** Primarily used for storage of data but can also be 'read' and the data extracted then stored.

→ **Stripe.** As above. Magnetic.

→ **Touch screen.** Sensors built into the screen allow taps to be calculated and fed back to the user as mouse movements.

→ **Track ball and glide point.** Two derivatives of the mouse. A track ball works in the same way as a mouse but the ball is moved rather than the whole unit. Glide point works like a touch screen.

Watch out!

Price *can* be attached to a bar code but this is rare – most systems use the reader to extract product data – this data will then relate to a product price held elsewhere.

Links

See Text manipulation page 58.

Checkpoint 1

What is RSI?

Action point

Make notes on these terms – don't concentrate on how they work but on the real life applications that they are most suited to.

Check the net

Some of the characteristics and operation of various I/O devices are discussed at: www.cit.ac.nz/smac/ns200/m4a.htm

Automated input

Some types of automated input are as follows:

- → **Data loggers.** Used to measure changes over time. For example, a logging device in a greenhouse may sense the temperature every two minutes for a three-day period, inputting the data without the need for human interaction.
- → **Movement sensors.** Used to detect movement or the proximity of objects, for example in burglar alarms and in 'intelligent robots'.

Output

There are a variety of output devices for different purposes:

- → **Printers.** These provide the user with a permanent 'hard' copy of their data. There are two basic types – impact and non-impact. Impact printers include **braille printers** that enable print-out in a format that can be utilised by the blind and **dot-matrix** printers that work by using pins to represent the shapes of letters or graphics. Non-impact print involves the use of **laser** or **inkjet** technology.
- → **Plotters.** These act very much like printers but are generally employed in production or architectural type applications when the pen on the arm of the plotter follows a programmed path to produce images (often lines).
- → **Visual Display Units.** VDUs or monitors that are used to give a graphical display of data. They do not provide a permanent means of display so some form of hard copy is usually required. Some VDUs can have touch sensitive screens of rapid access to information, i.e. tourists maps in garages.
- → **Sound.** This can either be the use of sound to enhance the computing experience or the use of sound as warning or to get the attention of the user.
- → **DVD** movies and sound, CDs music and data.
- → **Action.** Output via action involves the use of a reaction to an event such as the results of a data-logging system that measures temperature in a plant hothouse. When the temperature reaches a certain level, motorised windows open to help reduce the temperature and keep it within its limits or in machining (CAD/CAM), where a design on a screen triggers a machine to produce an item from a block or piece of material.

Exam questions   answers: page 24

An old OMR stock control system is being replaced. This system allows employees to check stock level regularly.

(a) Suggest *three* ways in which stock levels could be checked.

(b) Cost is one factor that determines the method of data collection – what other factors need to be taken into consideration?   (15 min)

Software – types and capabilities

Systems software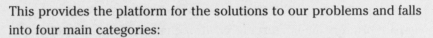

This is software that controls the way the computer functions. It creates an interface between the user and the hardware.

→ Operating system (see next section).
→ Utilities. File management, virus protection and accessories such as calculators and calendars.
→ Text editor. Can be used for writing batch files, or raw HTML.
→ Library programs. For frequently used tasks.

Could be an 'add-on' to your O/S or bought separately, e.g. Norton Disk Doctor, Nuts and Bolts or Management Tools.

Applications software

This provides the platform for the solutions to our problems and falls into four main categories:

→ **Textual** (e.g. word processors). Facilitates the manipulation and presentation of text.
→ **Numeric** (e.g. spread sheets). Processes, analyses and interprets numbers. Output can be textual, numeric, graphical or a combination of all three.
→ **Data handling** (e.g. databases). Can store, manipulate and manage various forms of data. Can be queried and analysed.
→ **Graphical** (e.g. presentational software). Facilitates the manipulation of graphics, text, sound, etc. and provides high quality output.

Such software can be obtained as either part of an integrated package or as discrete software items. Both types have distinct advantages and disadvantages, see table below.

		Integrated	Discrete
Advantages		Relatively inexpensive and widely available	More powerful
Advantages		Integrates well with others in suite – portability of data	Usually has more features and increased capability
Disadvantages		May never need some items in the suite	Integration is less straightforward
Disadvantages		May be missing some important advanced features	Costs more to buy

Bespoke v off-the-shelf ●●●

There are two main options when considering the method of obtaining your software. These are:

Bespoke

→ The software is designed and produced for you.
→ A perfect solution is produced for your problem.
→ Time and money is needed to produce it.
→ May not be flexible enough to cope with changes.

Off-the-shelf

Specialised purpose-built packages are available, e.g. accounts, tax-calculation.

→ They are usually well tested.
→ Have a large customer base with good levels of support.
→ May not exactly fit user's needs.
→ Relatively inexpensive.

There is, of course, the possibility of tailoring a generic applications package to the user's needs.

Program and translation ●●●

Software exists whose purpose is to produce software. This is called program software. It tends to be limited by its predetermined rules (syntax/semantics). The ability of a computer to be self-programming is a huge issue in the development of artificial intelligence and neural networking.

Software also exists whose purpose is translating programs into a format that can be read by machine, i.e. compilers, interpreters and intermediate code producers.

The jargon

Generic – general purpose, fitting the possible needs of many specific applications when manipulated.

Examiner's secrets

You may be faced with a scenario where you are required to put forward an argument for one method or another.

Checkpoint 3

Why would a home user purchase 'off-the-shelf' software rather than bespoke?

Don't forget

Your coursework will probably be based on tailoring a generic package to meet your end user's need – use your own experiences to highlight advantages and disadvantages!

Checkpoint 4

What does an interpreter application do?

Exam questions   answers: pages 24–5

1 An office worker has created a macro which imports data from one spreadsheet file to another and then performs some calculations. However, the macro fails to work as expected when it is used.
   (a) Explain the term 'macro' as used in the above description.
   (b) What could the office worker have done to reduce the chance of the macro failing when it was used?   (8 min)

2 A word processing package is used by both a technical author and an office secretary. The author uses it to produce scientific books, the secretary for letters to customers.
   (a) Describe *two* features of the word processing package that would be important to the author but not necessarily the secretary, explaining what they would be used for.
   (b) Describe *two* features of the word processing package that would be important to the secretary but not necessarily to the author, explaining what they would be used for.   (10 min)

Operating systems

The operating system is the core of the computer. It controls the way each machine works, handling everything from displaying data on the screen to managing peripheral interrupts, thus minimising the need for human interaction.

History ●●●

Key stages in the development of operating systems are as follows:

→ 1950s to mid-1970s. Operators keyed in machine codes, using binary switches. No operating systems were present.
→ Mid-1970s. To minimise operator-time wastage, batch operating systems were introduced for mainframes.
→ Late 1970s. ROM based O/S for personal computers as storage media took the form of unreliable audio tape.
→ 1981. The advent of the floppy disk led to Disk Operating System – a Microsoft product for IBM compatibles.
→ Early 1980s. Improvements in DOS made it compatible with hard disk storage heralding the advent of hierarchical file structures. Small improvements were made over the next five years but command line drivers still dominated.
→ Late 1980s. Apple Macintosh O/S developed (GUI) Windows to help the user navigate.
→ Late 1980s to early 1990s. A joint venture between Microsoft and IBM was launched, to produce the OS/2 multi-tasking windows environment. MS added on a graphical user interface to DOS not a true windows O/S.
→ Mid-1990s. The venture broke down – IBM developed OS/2 further. Meanwhile, Microsoft developed Windows 95. Many similar systems became available. Unix, a mainframe O/S began to gain popularity in the personal computing world, spawning Linux and other similar O/S for use on the PC.

The jargon

Peripheral – an additional hardware device, generally one that exists outside the casing of the base unit, i.e. printer, scanner, external drives.

Examiner's secrets

You do not need to know many specifics regarding the history of O/S. Make sure you can relate why O/S were developed, paying attention to the different user needs.

Take note

Apple's early GUI systems appealed to the creative industries (graphics and printing) who found GUI systems much easier to cope with than DOS. This has resulted in Apple being the industry's standard machine.

Checkpoint 1

What does GUI stand for?

The jargon

GUI – Graphic or Graphical User Interface.

Examiner's secrets

Make sure you know these purposes – it is an easy question to score well on if it comes up!

Purposes ●●●

→ **Interface.** Allows the user to correspond with the system either by commands or through a GUI.
→ **Memory management.** Ensures there is enough memory available to operate all functions successfully.
→ **Resource allocation.** The scheduling of time slots to different programs when more than one is being used. Also allocates input and output resources.
→ **Interrupt handling.** Every keystroke or message from a peripheral (for example) is an interrupt. The O/S keeps a track of these so that they do not prevent processes being completed.
→ **Backing store management.** The O/S controls the transfer of data from secondary to main memory. It also keeps a register of the disk so that free space and files can be located quickly.

Types

There are various types of operating systems, as follows:

Command line

→ A system that allows fast access to your files.
→ Knowledge of commands is required.

Graphical user interface (GUI)

→ The use of icons to represent the contents of files.
→ Quick access and results for novices.
→ Lie on top of a disk operating system. Complex file maintenance still needs to be undertaken via command line.

Windows

→ Also uses icons to represent file contents.
→ File maintenance support on board.
→ Utility software heavy, so much memory is required for seamless operation.
→ Multi-tasking, so operation time is reserved for work.

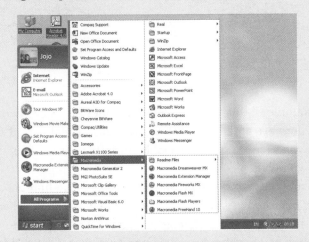

Exam questions   answers: page 25

'*Computers need an operating system. An enhanced GUI would probably help sell one.*'

(a) What is the function of an operating system?
(b) Give *two* reasons why an improved graphical user interface will be attractive to a systems administrator.   (8 min)

Checkpoint 2

Why is the term 'windows' used for operating systems?

Check the net

A great web site that explains O/S well. www.howstuffworks.com/operating-system.htm and an informative collection of research at www.tunes.org – search their site using 'Oses' as the keyword.

Checkpoint 3

Define the term 'icon'.

Checkpoint 4

What is the greatest advantage of a GUI-based O/S.

General and special purpose systems

At first glance, many systems would appear to have a single purpose. Looking deeper we can see that some systems are purpose built and others simply take on that appearance when in use.

The jargon

4GL – Fourth Generation Language.

Examiner's secrets

There is often a question about this topic – you will probably be asked to produce an argument that would be presented to an organisation's decision makers – come up with a range of advantages and disadvantages for both and you should be able get most of the marks on offer.

Checkpoint 1

State an advantage for using an application generator.

Application generators

As ICT has infiltrated society, so individual skills have become more flexible. Until the development of 4GLs, software development was the domain of programmers.

When purchasing software, the choices were:

→ Off-the-shelf. Too specific and restrictive if your purposes differed from those of the package.
→ Bespoke. Too expensive.

Various software houses saw an opening for shells of software systems, i.e., applications generators. These take the form of data handling, manipulation and presentation programs that can be crafted with minimal programming experience to produce a system that is fundamentally general purpose but when crafted takes on a specific role. They also go by the term generic software.

Many advanced features exist, including complex querying and report generation, charting and presentational options.

The following are examples of products from Microsoft and Lotus:

One example of this generic software could be an electronic diary system. There are a number of these systems available of the shelf. However, what makes them special is that the user can customise them to their own needs.

They can be set to be an email client, alone, or a fully interactive electronic personal organiser – integrating email, calendar, address book and note taker. The application can be set to carry out automatic actions, such as checking for email, and scanning the email for an appointment, then adding that appointment into the calendar. An alarm can then be set to remind the user that an appointment is approaching. All of these actions can be set through relatively simple changes, managed by 'wizards' or templates, making a generic application, specialised to a particular use for a particular user.

Special purpose systems

The hardware environment they occupy can generally define these systems. Taking a special purpose program out of context will lead to inoperation.

Special purpose hardware will allow little input from humans so instructions tend to be ROM-based.

These systems tend to be chiefly employed in the domestic appliance and industrial markets.

→ **Domestic appliances.** Logic preset into a microwave cooker will allow the preset cycles to be used in tandem with user-defined instructions.

→ **Industrial applications.** These systems are generally driven by the requirements of the products they work with rather than the system being developed and the business adapting to the system's capabilities.

One area that is being investigated by electronics companies is the integration of enormous amounts of special purpose systems, to produce a home that is suited to a particular user – room temperature and lighting, cooking of favourite meals, choice of entertainment – all working together to make the home more relaxing. There is also the industrial value of such technology – integrated manufacturing devices, automating the production of goods.

Checkpoint 2

Why are embedded systems used in household devices?

The jargon

Fuzzy Logic – software that works out probabilities of fact – not simply true or false, but partly true or partly false depending on a number of factors – fuzzy logic in washing machines is used to calculate the weight of clothing and then distribute only enough water to do the job effectively.

The jargon

Embedded systems are used extensively in both industrial and appliance systems – they hold their special software on ROM and are incorporated into the casing of the appliance.

Checkpoint 3

Program updates can be available on the Internet – why might this be useful to a washing machine user?

Exam questions   answers: pages 25–6

1   Application generators and report generators are available to increase the productivity of the end-user:
    (a) What is an application generator?
    (b) What is a report generator?
    (c) When would it be sensible to use each one?   (10 min)
2   A computer programmer needs to develop a system using an application generator, specifically a spreadsheet.
    (a) Suggest *two* reasons why an applications generator would be used.
    (b) Suggest *two* reasons why using an applications generator would not be a good idea.
    (c) Without using spreadsheet software in your answer, what are the main features of an applications generator?   (15 min)

Backup and security

The importance of an organisation's data cannot be underestimated. Loss of data can have effects ranging from cessation of business (in the most extreme cases), to less drastic, though still inconvenient effects for those better prepared.

Backup devices

Specific hardware exists for the safe creation of backups. The most common fall into three groups:

→ Disk drive – FDD, HDD, Zip, etc.
→ Tape streamer – DAT.
→ Optical writer – CDW, CDRW, DVDW.

Backup media

Magnetic media such as hard disks and floppy disks are still the most popular. These have been joined on the market by high compression disks such as Zip and Superdisk.

Disks are a popular format as they can store data without occupying much system space. Non-sequential or direct retrieval is possible, which means that disks are quick to use.

RAID allows data to be written simultaneously on two or more disks. Tape streamers use serial storage and so are not so quick at retrieval, but they can be used to store vast amounts of data – 8GB tape is not uncommon.

Both tape and disk tend to degrade with time, so a more permanent form of storage is desirable. Hence the invention and common use of compact disk!

→ Various types of CD exist. Some can be written to once and read many times (WORM), while others are re-recordable.
→ Magneto optical disks are a combination of rewritable backup format using lasers to write and magnetic heads to read.

Security methods

Different situations require different combinations of the following methods:

1 Disaster planning – ensure there is a plan and that it is tested to ensure it works.
2 Physical security
   → Install security doors with swipe cards, etc.
   → Use keyboard, desktop and printer locks – these secure items to immovable objects.
   → Location – ensure backups are kept off-site!
   → Safe – use of a safe is advisable – make sure it is waterproof and fire proof.

The jargon

RAID – Redundant Array of Inexpensive Disks.

Checkpoint 1

What does 'non-sequential' mean?

Exam tip

You may find yourself faced with a question requiring you to suggest a suitable backup strategy for a given situation. Make sure you read the situation carefully before selecting devices, media and strategy.

Check the net

An online presentation describing backup strategies can be found at: www.tutorials.beginners.co.uk/read/category/99/id/395

3 Logical security
→ Passwords, retina scanners, fingerprint decoders.
→ Virus checkers.
→ Access logs – help you track the activities of users.
4 Other security
→ Forced recognition – this is a document signed prior to computer use (usually part of an employment contract) that outlines conditions of computer use and the consequences of non-compliance.

Action point

Compile a list of different security methods and research products that have been developed to match these methods.

Checkpoint 2

Why should backups be taken of important data?

Exam questions   answers: pages 26–7

1 A company administers its business using a database system running on a network of PCs. This is used to process customer orders or log payments. Suggest backup strategies and their importance.
   (a) Suggest *two* reasons why it is wise to have a workable backup strategy.
   (b) Suggest *five* considerations for a backup strategy, illustrating each factor with an example.
   (c) Some data might still be lost if there was a system failure. Give *two* reasons why this might be the case.   (20 min)
2 At one time floppy disks were the medium for distributing software.
   (a) Where would it still be sensible to use a floppy disk for software distribution?
   (b) How, other than by floppy disk, can software be distributed? Give, with reasons, an example of when each one might be used.   (10 min)
3 A Surgery's information system holds program files; these are rarely changed, the database files however are changing constantly. Their backup strategy uses a tape storage device, and has the following characteristics:
   • Every evening a full back up is made.
   • Three sets of tapes are in use and are referred to as sets 1, 2 and 3.
   • Set 1 is used one evening.
   • Set 2 is used the next evening.
   • Set 3 is used the following evening.
   This sequence is then repeated, starting the next evening, with Set 1 again.
      A change has been suggested to improve this strategy. Give, with reasons, *four* changes that could be made.   (12 min)

Role of communications

Communications systems have altered all of our lives to some extent. Business people conduct themselves on a global scale, households can benefit from the use of communications, students have a new source for research.

Uses of global communications ●●●

There are many uses of global telecommunications.

→ Telephony – telephones, mobiles, fax, telex.
→ Analogue or digital.
→ Direct communication – duplex.
→ Touch-tone allows communication with a subsystem, e.g., enquiry systems in organisations with many departments.
→ Faxback service – half duplex.
→ Telex – can transmit legal documents, fax cannot.
→ Internet and Intranet.
→ Provides the computers for global network.
→ Hosts pages belonging to the www.
→ Electronic mail, bulletin boards.
→ Video conferencing – duplex.
→ Remote control of remote computers and equipment (e.g., for polar or space exploration).
→ Intranet – a collection of web pages and an e-mail facility for use within an organisation – can be local or global.

Entertainment/leisure
Television

→ Simplex – one way, televison is a broadcast media – it comes into the home, but does not carry anything back to the transmitter.
→ Can be analogue or digital – the television signals can be transmitted in one of two forms, digital a stream of 0s and 1s; or analogue – a wave.
→ Can be used to 'surf' – switching between channels, never really settling on any one.

Video/music on demand
Viewdata

→ Simplex pages of data, accessed via a TV – Ceefax, Oracle etc.; these are a bank of pages that can be called and displayed on a TV screen, but are not interactive.
→ Half duplex, used within the travel industry – Prestel, this allows simple interaction with the pages, the user can make changes and send those changes back to the sender.

Facilities offered by global communications ●●●

→ Teleconferencing.
→ Video conferencing.
→ E-commerce and teleworking.

Watch out!

A communications system does not have to use computers.

Checkpoint 1

Communication systems generally use the telephony system – when was the telephone invented?

Test yourself

Ask family members and friends if their household insurance company uses a touch-tone system on their customer reception service.

Watch out!

The Internet and www are not the same thing; www is a function of the Internet.

Checkpoint 2

With the advent of mobile communication devices such as mobile telephones, it is easier to contact people on the move. State two advantages of this technology.

Speed learning

Make definition cards of the terms 'simplex', 'duplex', and 'half duplex'. Attach at least two examples to each.

Test yourself

Make a list stating arguments for and against the assertion that global telecommunications provides a source of equal opportunity.

→ E-mail.
→ Remote access to research.
→ Equality of opportunity.

Informatics ●●●

Informatics is involved with the study of how ICT can best be used to work towards an information society. Most of the work in this area is centred on university research with the findings then influencing how ICT is incorporated into society.

Informatics is splitting up into specific areas of interest – there is a very active cell involved in health informatics, ensuring that ICT is exploited to best effect in health provision.

Telematics ●●●

Telematics is involved with the devices and methods used to get the information society working. It is about using ICT for learning and teaching. Web-based materials that allow the users or viewers to become immersed in the experience are the main use of telematics today. One of the most successful areas has been the telematic museum that allows virtual visitors to enjoy the artefacts and displays that a museum has without the need for expensive or time-consuming visits.

Recent developments ●●●

The three developments that will change the way we communicate this year could be: voice navigation on the Internet, wireless networks and e-paper and e-ink.

There are many others – see the 'Test yourself' in the margin.

Links

See Social impact in the next section (pages 38–9) for more information on this topic.

Check the net

Informatics and the information society are discussed in depth by City University, London:
www.soi.city.ac.uk
Exeter university have some interesting views on telematics at this site:
www.telematics.ex.ac.uk

Checkpoint 3

How can the health informatics help individuals?

Check the net

For innovations and the technology being developed now: www.bbc.co.uk/sn

Test yourself

Carry out directed research into the following communications developments:
Data compression (MP3/4);
Remote access and control;
Mobile communications, and especially Blue Tooth.

Checkpoint 4

What is voice recognition?

Exam questions   answers: pages 27–8

1   TV companies now offer new services because of digital TV. Interactive participative broadcasts and interactive teletext are two.
    What do you think the benefits of this technology might be?   (8 min)

2   A company has decided to make use of the Internet for advertising and organising their conferences.
    (a) State the purpose of the following Internet software:
         (i) browser (ii) editor (iii) e-mail software.
    (b) Explain *three* potential advantages for this company of using the Internet as opposed to conventional mail/telephone systems.   (15 min)

3   Technology has enabled use to operate on a global basis.
    Discuss this statement. Include in your discussion:
    •   Specific examples of facilities and/or tasks that make use of global communication systems.
    •   Specific examples of applications that make use of these facilities and/or tasks.
    •   The communications technology and/or techniques that have enabled this development.   (40 min)

Effect of hardware and software on human–

We have all experienced the use of unfamiliar hardware and software first hand. Much thought and design goes into the products before they reach us to help us interact with them as naturally as possible.

Checkpoint 1

Ergonomics must be considered to avoid discomfort or injury, why?

Links

See Health and Safety (pages 44–5).

Test yourself

Ask approximately five of your peers about the resolution to which they set their screens. What are their personal preferences and reasons?

Examiner's secrets

The examiner will be looking not only for definitions, but for demonstrations of analytical thought and reason.

Checkpoint 2

Why is the term 'Menu' used to describe parts of a GUI?

Links

See Design of the Human Computer Interface (pages 138–9).

Action point

Make notes on the two items in **bold** – try describing them without the use of diagrams!

Ergonomics

This refers to the physical interaction we have with a system. It covers the design of the hardware comprising the system and any other equipment we need to operate the system, e.g., is the desk the correct height? Is the keyboard designed to reduce strain on the hands and wrists?

The choice of a desktop or tower model for the casing of the base unit may be an important ergonomic decision for some. The choice will be partly made by the amount of space available.

If space is not an issue, other factors may preside:

→ Desktop – you can see the light on drive bays, maybe it reassures the user.
→ Tower – traditionally easier to work on the internal components.

. . . or maybe the user just prefers the look of one or the other!

Graphical user interface design

The first users of personal computers tended to be hobbyists who would tolerate using a *command line* to communicate with their system.

Over time the user base changed and computers were introduced wholesale into businesses. These users were by no means experts and needed help navigating through their systems. **Menu-driven interfaces** were created to meet this need.

Advantages of menu-driven interfaces:

→ Novices could navigate to their work.
→ Logical progression.
→ Input errors reduced as command line was not utilised.

Disadvantages of menu-driven interfaces:

→ Button title was not intuitive.
→ Tend to be structured so that direct access to a file on a sub-menu was not possible demonstrating their inherent inflexibility.

Nowadays, when faced with a software program, we tend to see icons, windows, a pointing device and we have access to pull-down or pop-up menus. These make up a **graphical user interface**. Fundamentally, word processing, spreadsheet programs, etc., will work without these items. They have been placed there and pre-programmed to help the user. They form the GUI.

computer interface

Advantages of graphical user interface:

→ Ease of use – builds confidence and competence.
→ Menus are available when needed.
→ Tend to be similar within 'families' of software. Builds transferable skills.
→ Provides a familiarity, which both aids and puts the user at ease.

Disadvantages of graphical user interface:

→ Uses lots of system resource.
→ Slower than both command line and menu systems.
→ The user does not see the process behind an icon, and therefore may have a false understanding of the process.
→ Lack of understanding may lead to the user not being able to perform simple tasks such as adding or deleting icons.

Human Factoring ●●●

Due to the increased use of software and GUIs there is a science of Human Factoring developing in industry.

Users are monitored as they interact with a device or application. The results are then used to influence further design and developments.

Some of the important factors that this evidence brings together may be difficult to gather by other means. The position of software buttons, colour schemes, text labelling, and other things which can make navigation around a web site intuitive, are very difficult to assess, yet it is easy to say when something is done poorly.

Prestigious company web sites are very carefully trialled before they go public, to ensure that users have a positive experience when using them; a negative experience can influence the likelihood of prospective customers or clients engaging with the company.

Check the net

Some interesting research into this field can be seen at this site: www.ergo.human.cornell.edu
Try searching using your favourite search engine, to find hits for human computer interaction as well as GUI.

Checkpoint 3

What does HCI stand for?

Exam questions   answers: page 28

A new stock control system has affected staff that work for a supermarket group. The workers are not used to computer systems.
However workers think the system is 'user friendly', except for one store.

(a) What do we mean by 'user friendly' software? Give *four* examples.
(b) Physical and psychological factors can influence how people interact with computers systems and these could have contributed to the poor reception of this system in that store.
   (i) Describe *two* such physical factors.
   (ii) Describe *two* such psychological factors.   (15 min)

Language group hierarchies and translation methods

There are many programming languages, each designed for specific purposes. Some are numerically based and provide sound platforms for mathematical or business software. Others are text based and allow for systems where use is not so strictly bound.

History

Both of the following are examples of machine-based, low-level languages:

→ Machine code – binary.
→ Assembly language – instructions are symbols, e.g., ADD, DIV, MULT and SUB and numbers are Hexadecimal or Octal to speed up processing.

Due to a need for portability of software between different machines, high-level languages were developed.

→ Easier to understand and code – commands are words and numbers are denary.
→ Speed up testing and debugging.

Checkpoint 1

Define the term 'binary'.

3GL and procedural design

→ Structured high level languages.
→ Sequences of commands defined and carried out, step by step.
→ Subject to strict syntax and semantic rules, e.g., Pascal, Fortran, C.

The jargon

Syntax – Structure.
Semantics – Meaning.

4GL and query language

→ Allow the user to add in functionality and develop solutions.
→ Started as a system to permit query, design and production of reports.
→ Current uses include application generators.
→ Many capabilities but with limits, e.g., Access database, Lotus 1-2-3, SQL.

Watch out!

In the end, all languages are translated into machine code for processing!

Checkpoint 2

What is the difference between 'platform-specific' and 'cross-platform'?

Non-procedural languages

→ Code does not tell the system how to perform.
→ Declarative – clauses that declare the problem or object, are fed in. Reaction is by query or in response to mouse clicks for example.
→ Can contain event-driven procedures – when event finishes, system waits for next event then carries it out. May be held as libraries or pre-programmed macros (e.g., right click button = pop-up menu).
→ Some examples of non-procedural languages are prolog for AI, C++, Visual Basic for windows based applications.

Action point

Research OOP and event-driven programming. How could these software development techniques be used in your coursework modules?

Translation methods ●●●

Getting the program into a machine-readable format is imperative. The translation method used will have an effect on the speed of execution so must be considered when choosing software. There are three methods available:

→ **Interpretation** – slow, translates line by line. Source code is interpreted every time the program is executed.
→ **Compilation** – compiles translated source code into a machine code object program. Requires one translation – subsequent executes use the object program.
→ **Intermediate code** – assembling high level to low level. Interprets the subcode when executing.

Computer-aided software engineering tool ●●●

CASE tools exist to help project development. Their capabilities range from documentation to code production.

Project management software is a good example. It is used to schedule work over a given project period and can display this in a variety of ways – on screen, via Gantt charts and via critical path diagrams. Other software exists to help with the declaration of entities and attributes and then takes this information as the basis for table structures.

Linkers and loaders ●●●

Used to link together programs that have been assembled separately.

Incorporate a library (common procedure) without needing to code into the program. This tool is especially convenient when working on large projects with many module developers.

Examiner's secrets

Ensure you can clearly define the difference between 'compiled' and 'assembled' software. The examiner may also be interested in your reasoning of why interpretation still exists when compilation is quicker.

Checkpoint 3

What is a Gantt chart?

Exam questions   answers: page 29

Vista is a high-level language, which a programmer wishes to use.
A systems administrator informs the programmer that there is no compiler for VISTA, only an interpreter.

(a) What is high-level language?
(b) Describe the essential difference between an interpreter and a compiler.
(c) Explain why this difference may be important to:
   The systems administrator.
   The programmer.   (20 min)

Answers
Hardware and software

Hardware – types and capabilities

Checkpoints

1 Personal Computer (PC), a self-contained computer system, consisting of input, and output devices, data storage and a central processing unit.
2 Standalone computers work independently, networked computers share data with other machines.
3 Advantages include speed, flexibility and reliability; disadvantages include cost, maintenance, vulnerability to viruses and crime.

Exam question

The advantages and disadvantages of using such a system, bearing in mind that the till has its own processor, are:
Advantages: Access to data speeds up and helps the customer (they can get faster service) and the spares managers, as they are keeping the customer serviced. All tills will keep their own records if the system fails.
Disadvantages: The initial cost of hardware is high, as is the maintenance.
Because the till may send data in small batches the server is not always up to date.

Examiner's secrets

A simple list of advantages and disadvantages is perfectly acceptable – if you want to heighten your chances of success, state the ICT reason for your answer and back it up with a short, real-life explanation.

Internal components

Checkpoints

1 Speed and volume of data transfer, the serial system allows a small amount of data to be transferred, parallel systems allow large amounts of data to be transferred at once.
2 Hot plugging – can be connected/disconnected when machine is on.
Hardware is automatically recognised, while plug system is uniform.

Exam questions

(a) New facilities such as sound or graphics can be provided, also a parallel port, network card, or modem, for example, will enable outside communications. Modifications may have to be made to the hardware subsystems and the operating systems.
(b) Plug and play systems automatically detect new facilities and make the necessary alterations.
(c) Time consuming consultations with technical documentation would have to be made by the systems administrator if plug and play was not available. Who would then alter the operating system and hardware manually?

Input and output devices

Checkpoints

1 Repetitive strain injury.
2 Two states – on/off, hi/lo, yes/no.
3 Hard disk on newer systems, DVD on older systems.
4 Bitmaps are grids of data describing a graphical image, each piece of data describes location, colour, hue, etc.

Exam questions

(a) A combination of barcode readers and barcodes could be used, input via keyboard; a portable device could be used, hand held data capture device (either barcode-reader based or keypad based); optical character recognition, voice recognition or smart chips plus a smart chip reader.
(b) Various factors will have an effect on choice including:
 • Quantity of data – the size of the operation.
 • Quality of data required – depends on the quality of information that is required as a result of the system.
 • Diversity of stock – it may not be possible to apply one data capture method to all of the products you hold.
 • Diversity of sites – the location or the nature of the site: If location is a factor then a stock control system that can be administered at a distance will be attractive. If the nature of the site is a factor (e.g. crude oil plant) then a system that requires little human interaction may be attractive.
 • Staffing level available – staff may be required to have face-to-face contact, therefore chose EPOS type system linked to stock control.
 • Level of system equipment.
 • Ease of use.
 • Throughput – timescale involved – a batch system will not need constantly updated stock control, but a catalogue shop will.
 • Level of detail required in data capture – accuracy required.

Software – types and capabilities

Checkpoints

1 Easy for a user to work with, makes complicated actions easier to perform.
2 Textual and graphical.
3 Cost, general use, rather than specific tasks-based applications.
4 Translates software into a form that can be understood by another piece of software, to ensure data communication.

Exam question 1

(a) To enable a task to be repeated quickly a series of keystrokes are recorded for future playback, a sub-routine that may be used sometimes or a commonly occurring procedure, e.g. templates that are often used. A set of instructions that may be called either by name or automatically, in response to another action.

(b) It would appear that minimal testing occurred during creation of the system and if carried out, this would have minimised the chance of failure.

The system was not thoroughly tested whilst it was being made; had this been carried out failures could have been minimised.

Testing strategies could include:

- To see if the macro works – unit testing but in isolation, i.e. step-by-step, macro should be written first with exact data test and move on, then write a macro to open the new sheet, test and move on, then write a macro that inserts the data, test and move on, etc.
- Integration testing – testing the macro but in its environment.
- Dummy data could be used to test if systems can handle data sets in the volumes required.
- User acceptance testing.

Exam question 2

(a) Any *two* from the following list:

- To cope with the range of words used and possible interpretations of the words used a thesaurus would be needed.
- Due to the nature of the technical authors' subject – special symbols could be used.
- To ensure that the spell check only picked up incorrect words not simply unusual or special words a technical dictionary would be needed.
- Page numbering – for indexing and table of contents purposes as well as cross referencing purposes.
- Auto format for subheadings – to help reduce the time taken to produce the work.

(b) Any *two* from the following list:

- Standard letter templates – again as a time saving device.
- Mail merge – to automate a time-consuming job that needs a personal touch.
- Images – an author would not be expected to put images in – a publisher would.

Operating systems

Checkpoints

1 Graphical user interface.
2 Data is displayed in rectangular boxes, similar to windows, they are a way of 'seeing' what is going on.
3 Small graphical image used to represent an action.
4 User does not need to know programming language, or be able to program.

Exam questions

(a) History – to help reduce the amount of work involved in computer use, operating systems were developed. Their basic task is to automate routine functions and ensure that the system is operating and co-ordinating as well as it can.

From the following mention at least two or more:

- Provides an interface – allows the users to operate it and use their programs.
- Handles interrupts.
- Manages memory.
- Allocates resources.

(b) Historically, the better the GUI (graphical user interface) design the *easier the system is to use* (the secret of Apple-Macs' early success). The systems administrator would be able to concentrate his or her energy on the more difficult problems that users are having, as good GUI design irons out many simple queries. Before Windows all problems where resolved in DOS. This in turn would *enhance the image of the systems administrator*.

General and special purpose systems

Checkpoints

1 Application generators allow a user to put together predefined procedures to produce a required outcome, this saves the user having to start from scratch each time a new application is required.
2 Users will not need to be able to program the device.
3 New soap powders or textiles may mean differences in washing techniques.

Exam question 1

(a) The user can manipulate the structure to fit their needs; generic software called an application generator is used, allowing a solution to be crafted with minimal programming expertise.

(b) Report generators software takes data, and from that devises reports. It deals with presentation of the data in a way that does not involve complex querying of the data by the user.

(c) To produce a solution to a business problem that is specific to an organisation an application generator would be used, i.e., a package does not exist to purchase off-the-shelf.

Example: A spreadsheet solution for calculating the amount of driving hours that long-haul and short-haul drivers can legally do during journeys without a break. This will be specific to this industry.

To process large amounts of data a report generator would be used. Data could then be presented in an easily understandable fashion.

A report derived as a result of replies to questionnaires would be a good example. Data would be fed in, field by field, and a query attached to the system. Reports showing the extracted information would be produced.

Exam question 2

(a) An applications generator exists within a development environment that provides a range of complex facilities and functions that can be integrated into the application being developed, for example spell checker, referential integrity checker, selection of predefined user interfaces. The development time is minimised due to the high level in initial functionality.

(b) The customer will have to own a copy of the generator, for example the spreadsheet software, whereas an application developed into complied code has no extra software overhead.

Using a general purpose high level language gives maximum flexibility from a specification point of view.

(c) The answer to this will depend on the amount of development experience you have had – stick to something you know for instance a WYSIWYG web development program or a database.

Backup and security

Checkpoints

1 Data can be stored in different sectors of a disk, then retrieved without loss.

2 Machine damage or failure, theft of equipment, archiving for security.

Exam question 1

(a) Two main reasons:

The organisation could lose money – lost data will need to be replaced – sotfware may need to be replaced or reinstalled.

Data must be held secure if this is lost through lack of proper breach of the Data Protection Act in which the organisation is bound to ensure that all data held is secure – loss through lack of adequate backup would be seen as negligence.

(b) Five considerations from the following:

How frequently you backup. The type of business you are in depends on how often you backup. Online systems selling tickets, for example; gas bill production could be backed up less frequently because the data contained will alter less frequently.

The number of generations to be kept. Some businesses backup each day, month or year. Re-creation of lost files and data will normally be possible using this strategy.

The medium used for storage. Two factors to think about here are – cost, space and method of data retrieval. If data that is being stored is of a non-sequential nature, a medium offering random access will be most appropriate, e.g., CD RW or WORM. On the other hand if the data does not require random access or cost is a serious consideration, then a magnetic medium such as tape would be appropriate.

Locations for storage of the backup. Preferably out of the building, ideally in a fireproof and watertight crush-resistant safe.

The plan's effectiveness. Testing is the only solution. Faults found need to be addressed immediately.

Responsibility for the plan. It must be perfectly clear who is responsible, they must be easily identifiable. So that the time between loss and getting the plan into action for retrieval is as small as possible also, so that any breaches in procedure can be put right by those responsible for them, not necessarily those who actually perform the backup.

(c) System failure and backup time may be incompatible, e.g., failure could start five minutes before scheduled backup.

Lost data may be corrupted to the extent that it cannot be salvaged.

Exam question 2

(a) For example, distribution of a software 'fix' or printer driver.

File distributed is small, i.e., less than 1.44 Mb or 2 Mb. Suitable for people using 'older' equipment, i.e., the floppy disk is still universal. Very little is produced on floppy disk because backup can be done on CD, larger 120 Mb disk, zips etc., which can hold many times more information than a floppy.

Sometimes it is necessary to boot from the media prior to installation of CD driver, e.g., installation of an OS. Floppy disk holds authentication information.

(b) CD-ROM
  - Easy to distribute and mass-produce.
  - Cannot be altered or interfered with.
  - Can hold a large amount of information.
  - Quick to access.
  - Fairly robust.

  Internet site or bulletin board
  - If you registered you can access upgrades.
  - Transfers the distribution costs to the end user.
  - Upgrades/'fixes' are available to all when posted to the site.
  - Manufacturers can send demo versions with a limited life for trial.

  E-mail
  - Can be used to send drivers/'fixes' to registered software owners.
  - Reduces distribution costs.
  - No media costs.
  - Instant.

Exam question 3

Changes are *italic*, reasons are indented:

System files only need backup prior to systems upgrades.
  - Reduce backup time.
  - A hospital system must never be down.

Separate procedures, systems, media and devices form backing-up system/program files and database files.
  - Will reduce the demand on storage capacity.
  - Occasional dump of database to disk while online.
  - Without going offline the dump can be backed up.

A weekly backup to tape is needed.
- Data errors will overwrite good data in three days if not discovered.

Raid array to facilitate online backup.
- The time the system is unavailable will be reduced. A hospital's system cannot afford to be offline.

Keep off site master/keep in a fireproof safe.
- Added security.

Medium-term full backup to CD/dump to CD.
- More reliable than tape.
- If a data error is not detected within three days it will be impossible to restore from backup.

Set up a live mirror server to act as backup on the network.
- Improve recovery time after data loss.

Live backup to another machine across the network.
- Faster recovery from disaster.

Employ software solution to enable online backup. If offline time is a problem, find a software solution to enable online backups to take place.
- To reduce down time/hospital system must never be down.

Planned testing of tapes by restoring them.
- To ensure media/strategy is OK.

Maintain a backup log.
- To keep records of failure in backup process.

Use compression.
- To reduce the backup time or storage media space.

Role of communications

Checkpoints

1 In 1876 by Alexander Graham Bell.
2 Emergency contact, avoid missing appointments, carry out meetings while out of the office, pass information when needed.
3 Central data storage of important health information, meaning patients can have their records checked quickly. Avoids misdiagnoses.
4 The ability of a computer system to learn the voice pattern of a user, then decode spoken instructions, and use them as data.

Exam question 1

The benefits are:
- Freedom of choice.
- Access to personalised information.
- Loss of national viewership for common programmes.
- Different views on sports events.
- Video-on-demand.

Exam question 2

(a) (i) Internet browsers are used to read, view and browse information on the Internet.

(ii) An Editor is for Internet users to create or edit pages for hosting on the web.

(iii) **E-mail software** – electronic communications can be sent by the user – either one-to-one or one-to-many.

(b) The examples below represent acceptable answers in an examination:
- Time. The market for this company is international, therefore, time differences make phones calls difficult. Using e-mails means that time difference problems are eradicated as e-mails can be picked up when convenient.
- Target audience. Conventional mailing systems may not reach these people, they may be very mobile. E-mail messages can be directed to individuals and picked up anywhere in the world. They are received independent of location or time. For example mobile phone technology is now a commonplace medium for receiving e-mails.
- Because e-mails can carry images as well as text this allows for a quick response to requests, for example, for news items or photos for newspapers. Saves staff time, no stamps, franking or postroom operations. Not likely to get lost.
- Adverts are accessible to a wide audience at minimal cost to the producer. They can be translated by online readers or made available in other languages as appropriate. Conventional printing of adverts and subsequent mailing is expensive.
- Cost. One message can be prepared and sent simultaneously at a cost of a local phone call – this would help to reach the international clientele.

Exam question 3

Examples of facilities and/or tasks that make use of communications systems:
- E-mail.
- EDI – electronic data interchange, e.g., for exam entries or corporate billing systems.

- Viewdata, Prestel or Ceefax.
- Closed user groups.
- In commercial use – distributed databases, online software support, technical support lines.
- In research fields – online databases, bibliographies.
- Electronic diaries.
- Telecommuting.
- Conferencing – both tele and video.
- Bulletin boards.
- Chat lines.

Examples of applications that make use of these facilities and/or tasks:
- *Finance*: ATMs, EFT, electronic clearing houses, online enquiry systems.
- *Sales*: POS, telemarketing, airline/hotel reservations, online order processing, credit card payment/authorisation.
- *Manufacturing*: process control, CIM – computer integrated manufacturing.
- *Human resource management*: personnel enquiry, application tracking, teleconferencing.

Or any suggestions about internal e-mail systems, etc.

Communications technology and/or techniques that have enabled this development:
- OSI approach to communications.
- Local Area Networks.
- Wide Area Networks.
- Gateways.
- Satellite links.
- Fibre optic technology.
- Protocols.
- Microwave systems.
- PABXs.
- Fax.
- Telephone.
- Superdata highways.
- Modem.

Possible problems in the technology:
- Lack of standards.
- Incompatible architecture.
- Small scale planning of LANs.
- Local need v organisation need.
- Security, hacking and viruses.

Effect of hardware and software on human–computer interface

Checkpoints

1 If devices are poorly designed the user will find them difficult to use, this can cause repetitive strain injury (RSI), or other problems.
2 A list of options from which the user chooses, like a menu in a restaurant.
3 Human Computer Interaction.

Exam questions

(a) Any four from the following;
- Intuitive to use.
- Command, menus etc. in familiar places on screen – similar menu structure to other packages.
- Ability to customise toolbars/menus.
- Help readily available online.
- Context sensitive help.
- Shortcuts available for expert users.
- Effective diagnostic messages on screen.
- Use of wizards to assist with complex tasks.
- Well suited to task – not unnecessarily complicated.

(b) (i) *Physical factors*:
- Position of screen/lighting – always visible and not facing windows/avoiding glare or reflections.
- Arrangement of seating – adjustable level for chairs.
- Work patterns – ability to take frequent breaks.
- Ergonomics of hardware – problems such as RSI, mention of keyboard design or wrist rests, etc.
- Choice of colour schemes – the effect of colour blindness to certain colours.
- Sound effects associated with tasks – problem in a noisy environment or for people with hearing difficulties.

(b) (ii) *Psychological factors*:
- A different set of peer pressures may exist in this store – for example, the manager at this store is against the new system.
- Different background or experience – these users may previously have used a different system to those in the other stores.
- Different satisfaction level/degree of familiarity with previous system – may have been using the old system longer.
- Strong ICT phobia/willingness to accept an ICT solution in this store.
- Different social context in this store – maybe this store is in the US/Europe, etc.
- Low user self-confidence – if many staff feel unable to cope, this may build to create dissatisfaction.
- Sound effects associated with tasks – initially helpful, could become irritating, etc.
- Choice of colour schemes – different colour combinations can affect mood or attitude towards the system.
- HCI complexity may frustrate expert users, because of help given to novice users.

Language group hierarchies and translation methods

Checkpoints

1 Using only 1s and 0s as a counting system.
2 Platform-specific only works on one type of machine. Cross-platform works on different types of machine.
3 A method of recording when actions are planned to take place, using calendar data in a graphical format.

Exam questions

(a) A programming language that is relatively easy for a human to understand.
It requires translation into machine code, before it is executed.
It can be procedural or non-procedural in its structure.

(b) A compiler turns a high-level language program into a logically equivalent run file, that can then be executed by the target processor without any reference to the source language. An interpreter executes the program statement by statement from the source code.

(c) *Systems administrator*
Use of an interpreter will take more processor and storage (the source code of the program has to be present) resources.

Programmer
The availability of an interpreter can greatly ease the development process, as there is likely to be a reduced time between source code modifications and an executed result. One the other hand, once development is complete, the programmer is concerned that the product executes as fast as possible and that the distribution of compiled code is a much easier and secure process.

Revision checklist
Hardware and software

By the end of this chapter you should be able to:

1	Confidently offer a definition for the terms, hardware and software.	Confident	Not confident **Revise** pages 4 and 10
2	Give a potted history of the development of the home PC.	Confident	Not confident **Revise** page 4
3	Describe the terms, EPOS, EFTPOS and e-commerce as well as suggest appropriate scenarios for their use.	Confident	Not confident **Revise** page 5
4	Have a working knowledge of each listed component in a microprocessor.	Confident	Not confident **Revise** page 6
5	Know when each input device should be used.	Confident	Not confident **Revise** page 8
6	Know the difference between systems and applications software and give examples.	Confident	Not confident **Revise** page 10
7	Argue the case for bespoke v off-the-shelf applications software (and vice versa).	Confident	Not confident **Revise** page 11
8	Know the differences between the categories of input and output devices.	Confident	Not confident **Revise** pages 8 and 9
9	Offer situations where specific devices should be used for input or output.	Confident	Not confident **Revise** pages 8 and 9
10	Describe the principal roles of an operating system.	Confident	Not confident **Revise** page 12
11	Define the terms, 'command line', 'GUI' and 'Windows'.	Confident	Not confident **Revise** page 13
12	Know what is meant by a special purpose system.	Confident	Not confident **Revise** page 15
13	Understand the importance of backup and security.	Confident	Not confident **Revise** pages 16 and 17
14	Offer a range of backup and security solutions depending on the nature of the business.	Confident	Not confident **Revise** pages 16 and 17
15	Have a coherent knowledge of the role of communications.	Confident	Not confident **Revise** pages 18 and 19
16	Describe the differences between the Internet and an intranet.	Confident	Not confident **Revise** page 18
17	Define the term ergonomics.	Confident	Not confident **Revise** page 20
18	List the advantages and disadvantages of GUI over command line or menu-based systems.	Confident	Not confident **Revise** pages 20 and 21
19	Offer a short history of programming language development.	Confident	Not confident **Revise** pages 22 and 23
20	Display knowledge of a range of CASE tools.	Confident	Not confident **Revise** page 23

Ethics, law and social impact

Systems that have a profound influence on people's lives are always open to abuse. In order to ensure that information and communication technology and the professionals involved in ICT are not open to criticism of unethical behaviour, certain structures are being put in place. The relatively new area of ICT can be seen as a legal minefield, especially as our legal system works on precedent, so laws and conventions regarding legality and illegal behaviour have been developed with one area of most concern – the protection of the individual's data. The development of the Information Society and its effects are also areas for consideration.

Exam themes

→ Information – its value, importance and control

→ Information as a commodity

→ The capabilities and limitations of ICT

→ Information Society and the social impact of ICT

→ ICT professionals and their use of information

→ The legal framework and health and safety aspects

Topic checklist

○ AS ● A2	OCR	EDEXCEL	AQA
Control of information	○		○
Value and importance of information	○		○
Capabilities and limitations of information and communications technology	●		○
Social impact	○	○●	○
Information and the professional	○		○
Legal framework	○		○
Health and safety	○		○

Control of information

Information is data, which has meaning. Data can be collated, bought and sold and has become an important aspect of successful business. Indeed, many organisations exist that have the buying, processing and selling of data as their only source of business.

Use of information as a commodity ●●●

Data on its own is not much use to an individual or company, but when that data has been analysed and manipulated it can prove to be extremely valuable. Various organisations deal in information as their main product. This can prove very useful to other organisations as they can purchase the information, rather than seeking it themselves.

→ Information can aid decision-making, e.g., reward card schemes in commerce help store management track buying habits for certain sectors of their market. Product introduction could then be based on the observation of these trends. Information from residential property builders could aid decisions about new school locations. New houses = children = education.
→ Information helps organisations to obtain and maintain competitive advantage.
→ Some organisations exist whose chief product is information, for example the Press Association based in Leeds.

Unfortunately there are some uses to which information can be put that are not so well thought of – e-mail spammers buy and sell e-mail addresses. These lists are then used by the spammers to send junk e-mail.

Obligations placed on the holder ●●●

→ Data is subject to restrictions within the Data Protection Act, if the content is more than simply names and addresses held for distribution purposes.
→ Data should be corrected if found to be inaccurate.
→ Data subjects must be made aware of your interest to sell information on to any third party – EU Directive 1995 – this consent is usually sought when obtaining the information.

Checkpoint 1

State one advantage to the retailer for the use of 'reward cards'.

The jargon

EU Directive – EU Directive on the protection of individuals with regard to the processing of personal data and on the free movement of such data 1995.

Checkpoint 2

Why would a company wish to purchase data from a data supplying company?

Check the net

The government actively encourages the public to keep up to date with freedom of information developments – take a look at this site: www.homeoffice.gov.uk and then search for 'freedom of information'.

Access to information

Any organisation holding information that relates to an individual or organisation is bound by various laws, including the Data Protection Act. However these laws are only applicable to companies in this country. There are international rules, but these are very difficult to enforce as not all countries have signed up to them.

→ Personal information must be made available.
→ A fee is usually attached – this should be reasonable, e.g., £5–£20.
→ If inaccuracies are found, they must be corrected.
→ If alteration does not occur, redress can be sought via the Data Protection Act and the Data Commissioner.
→ Failing that, civil action may be taken for compensation.
→ Personal information that constitutes part of an investigation on behalf of the police, military or government is not available for access.

Regulation of Investigative Powers Act 2000

This act of parliament relates to the control of information that is passed through a variety of communications channels. It permits certain, registered, individuals/bodies to intercept correspondence and access it. It has been a controversial law from the start and there is a huge amount of opinion published on the web.

Take note

Freedom of information can be obtained if it relates directly to you.
Information can be obtained by your legal representative, e.g., solicitor, accountant.

Checkpoint 3

Describe why the interception of e-mail, or other electronic communication, by certain approved bodies can be justified.

Examiner's secrets

Controversial, current ICT-related laws can be used as the focus for extended answers in the exam. Make sure you have a good knowledge of all the laws that affect ICT.

Exam questions   answers: page 46

Stored information about individuals is regarded as a commodity these days, to be bought and sold where possible. Information can be obtained in a variety of ways.

1   How could companies go about obtaining this type of information?
2   The latest method of obtaining information about individuals is to buy space on the appropriate websites, hoping viewers will fill in the survey forms as they pop up at random.
    What advantages does this system have over previous ones?   (10 min)

Checkpoint 4

State two reasons for the need for data protection legislation.

Value and importance of information

The importance and value of information depends on its use. If it is a core part of a business, then it will be of great importance. Its value and importance becomes especially pertinent if it becomes lost, incorrect or out of date.

The value of information as a commodity ●●●

Information can often be a commodity in its own right – to be bought and sold according to its market value, for example the use of residential house building. Information as the basis of opening new schools needs little more work other than finding out if the houses are being marketed at singles, currently childless couples or families.

→ Singles – possibly no school required. Houses not large enough for families.
→ Childless couples – may be moving to a larger home to have children = primary school.
→ Families – may have older kids = secondary school.

Information allows you to create categories and best fit.
It can be sold for financial gain.
The lack of information can lead to lost opportunities.

Lifestyle information ●●●

This is a specific type of information used to target patterns and 'types' of consumer.

→ Your household, family structure and income.
→ Details about your home.
→ Hobbies and pastimes.
→ Can lead to marginalisation of individuals – everyone must fit a category.

Effect of incorrect information ●●●

Information may be stored which is incorrect. Usually this is unintentional and an organisation that uses that information is open to redress by legislation; however, this can also have an effect on the organisation and the individual:

On the organisation

→ Bad decisions can be made.
→ Unable to meet customer demands.
→ Waste of resources, e.g., over-production of food, etc.
→ Could lead to physical danger, e.g., incorrect emission-level information being used as a guideline for a factory.

Checkpoint 1

Describe why 'lifestyle' information can be useful to a supermarket chain.

Action point

Can you find an example where lack of information led to a serious lost opportunity?

Test yourself

Who should take ultimate responsibility for the effects of incorrect information? The producer, for negligence? Or the user for blind compliance?

On the individual

→ Affect credit rating – unable to obtain loans, mortgages, etc.
→ Lead to damaged reputation.
→ Could affect employment, e.g., inaccurate criminal record.
→ Could prove life threatening, e.g., incorrect medical information.
→ Could expose vulnerable individuals to criminals.

Cost of ensuring information complies with law ●●●

Organisations must comply with legislation if they are to be seen as trustworthy; however, less reputable companies may try to avoid compliance by working from overseas bases, where different rules, sometimes less rigorous, apply.

→ Registration on the data protection register – small annual fee.
→ Personal freedom – prison sentences have been awarded for non-compliance.
→ Loss of good reputation.
→ Loss of business/customers.

Checkpoint 2

Explain why 'credit rating' can be important to an individual.

Exam questions   answers: page 46

Citizens depend on democratic governments to provide a range of services based on information they have been given.

This information often comes from data collected by specialist companies who analyse the data.

(a) Discuss a negative effect that could result from incorrect information being given.
(b) How could the information be provided incorrectly?
(c) What safeguards could the companies put in place to minimise mistakes?

(15 min)

Check the net

Search the web for sites relating to the Data Protection Act and the Information Commissioner.

Capabilities and limitations of information and

ICT can be used in every aspect of our lives. It is capable of making our lives easier (as it can tackle administrative burdens, etc.) and safer, in undertaking dangerous jobs for us. There are however limitations set, some by the users, some by the current technology.

Quality of information

Capabilities of ICT are limited by the quality of information, for example, mail shots of product information regarding a new range of children's videos to previous customers is a great marketing tool – if you have ensured that data collection included questions relating to householder's children's dates of birth – this is value-related to the relevance of information.

Quality information is that which is:

→ Brief.
→ Accurate.
→ Up-to-date.
→ Relevant.

Information that does not fulfil these criteria could mean that decisions made could be based upon the wrong data. Out-of-date information is often blamed for mistakes. However, nearly all data is date-related, so it should be easy to ensure that it is always up-to-date.

Management tool

There are software applications that are mentioned elsewhere in this book, that can be used as management tools, these can:

→ Aid decision-making
→ Make better use of resources:
 → Jobs that can be done by computer.
 → Jobs that need the human touch, e.g., using a medical diagnosis program in a busy accident and emergency department will help the staff decide on priorities for treatment.

Most organisations of any note will have a dedicated system that is used to control the information they deal with. They have become such key corporate tools that businesses grind to a standstill when their MIS are offline.

Human reliance

Some effects on human reliance are:

→ Loss of skills – for example the loss of simple mathematical skills due to the reliance on calculators.
→ Inability to make routine decisions without consulting system which can have an addictive effect demonstrated through social inability to make many decisions.

Checkpoint 1

Web marketing – web surveying will become commonplace with survey companies buying space on the appropriate web sites. Why would organisations such as Microsoft use the tool?

Checkpoint 2

Managers of multinationals now consider their worldwide intranets to be management tools. Staff reports and personal data can be sent and received via this software. State one advantage of this system.

The jargon

MIS – Management Information Systems.

Test yourself

Get each member of your group to bring in mail shots sent over the period of one week. Analyse them to see if the money spent on obtaining names and information was worthwhile.

communications technology

→ Special circumstances may not be considered, as operators are unable to over-ride presets, leading to inaccurate data (see 'example').

Benefits of ICT systems ●●●

As ICT has developed over time, more and more systems have been created. Many of these systems have created new facilities or jobs but many more have been created to replace systems carried out by humans.

The main benefit of using an ICT-based system over a human one is that there is a guarantee that the same process will be carried out time and time again without any loss in quality and without the operator becoming bored.

The ICT-based systems not only offer these attributes but also:

→ Fast processing.
→ Huge storage.
→ Powerful search facilities.
→ Real-time processing.
→ Tracking and feedback.

ICT systems have often been seen as the great solution for society's problems – however they can create difficulties as well. These disadvantages need to be balanced by the advantages. Installing a computer-operated system may mean higher quality results from that process, but staff morale may decrease, making quality results more difficult to attain in other parts of the process.

Example

A common feature in many insurance company systems, when giving a quote is to ask about residency – if not born in the UK, it is assumed that the driver learned to drive outside the UK. Fair enough if they did – the DVLA needs to ensure that all drivers are competent on UK roads – but if the driver learned in the UK, why are they then penalised with slightly higher premiums? In order to override this built in feature, the operator either has to lie about the driver's place of birth or get a supervisor to override the preset 'load' of increased premium! Not much scope for initiative!

The jargon

Real-time processing – transactions that have an immediate effect, e.g., update stock levels, make airline seat reservations, update pulse rates on hospital monitors.

Exam questions   answers: pages 46–7

1   It is now thought that some specialist ICT companies can produce software that out-performs the professionals.
    Suggest three features of such a system that have allowed them to out-perform their human counterparts.   (10 min)
2   The failure of some ICT systems could be disastrous in our society because we are so dependent on them working well.
    Give *two* different examples of ICT systems that would cause havoc if they failed.   (6 min)

Social impact

The Information Society is something we are all part of. It governs the way we communicate, learn, work and live. The impact that our use of ICT has on society is not always obvious. Some individuals have no access to computers – are they missing out? Is there too much reliance on ICT – should we encourage more book reading?

Check the net

The Information Society has spawned a vast number of interest groups – keep up to data at this site: www.connected.org where you will find a fascinating e-magazine.
The government has its own website dedicated to the Information Society and is well worh a visit at: www.isi.gov.uk

The jargon

CBD – Central Business District.

Checkpoint 1

Describe how the Open University has had a positive role in equality of opportunity.

Example

Europe's first Internet home has been built in Watford. This house can be controlled from anywhere in the world. The manufacturers claim you can check the house for burglars, check the children or feed the cat!

Employment

→ Teleworking – working from home and communicating electronically has led the way in changes to work location.
→ Call centres are generally located away from CBDs.
→ Patterns of work – many industrial systems are best utilised twenty-four-hours-a-day and work patterns have changed to reflect this.
→ Changes in work type – a move away from the traditional manufacturing base to the service base. Many manufacturing tasks can be undertaken by robots but call centres still need humans.

Education

→ Equality of opportunity due to distance learning – e.g., Open University using MMPCs to communicate lectures to students and work back to lecturers.
→ Multi-media has led to the realistic introduction of computer aided/assisted learning (CAL). Students can learn at their own pace, e.g., virtual schools for child actors in the US.
→ Resources – students can share ideas with others anywhere in the world. The Internet can prove a useful research tool when used properly.

The idea is not to *replace* the teacher but to *reinforce* the learning objective set.

Social interaction

→ New modes of communication – e.g., chat-rooms, e-mail, videoconferencing, texting.
→ Less need to actually be in the presence of those in the conversation.
→ Less physical activity – hours chatting online are hours lost exercising.

Benefits to people with special needs ●●●

→ Opens up lines of communication and possibly friendship opportunities.
→ Equality of access – stairs don't pose an obstacle to wheelchair users at an online auction. Total or partial blindness is insignificant when your scanner software reads out the news.
→ Shopping – more choice than from catalogues, if you are unable to leave your home – delivery of large objects means you don't have to manoeuvre them yourself.
→ Work – teleworking is ideal as employers' resources and restrictions won't apply at home.
→ Organisation and presentation for sufferers of dyslexia.
→ Independence and self-reliance.

Processing of waste ICT resources ●●●

Every year millions of tons of used ICT equipment are scrapped. Much of the casing materials could be recycled as could many of the metals used on internal components. However, this rarely happens and non-biodegradable waste is emptied into landfill sites. Many manufacturers now take it upon themselves to redress this balance.

Checkpoint 2

Describe why it is important to withhold your e-mail, or other personal details in a chat-room.

Take note

Voice recognition software means spelling, languages or some special needs need no longer be a barrier for communicating.

Take note

Produce a list of ICT equipment that manufacturers claim can be recycled – use this to form some personal opinions about the efforts currently being made to 'clean-up the act'.

Exam questions   answers: pages 47–8

1   Some medical consultants are being beaten by their computers when diagnosing illnesses.
    Internet self-diagnoses is becoming commonplace.
    Discuss the social, moral and legal implications of such systems.   (10 min)
2   'The Internet is changing the way we shop.'
    Discuss this statement. Include in your discussion:
    •   The types of organisation likely to advertise on such systems.
    •   The capabilities and limitations of such systems for this activity.
    •   The potential security risks for the customers in using such systems.
    •   The organisational impact of such systems.
    •   The social impact of such systems.   (40 min)
3   A company is updating it's word-processing software.
    State *one* problem disabled people might have using the new word-processing package and describe a software solution to the problem.
                                                    (5 min)

Information and the professional

The safe use and distribution of information is dependent on the individuals who have access to it. The personal characteristics of these individuals could influence the way they do the job. ICT professionals find themselves in a position of trust that could see unscrupulous individuals exploit the less knowledgeable for vast sums of money or ineffective products/solutions.

> "In common with professional bodies in other fields, the BCS has formulated its own rules as a Code of Conduct to define the behaviour expected of BCS members in everyday professional life."
>
> British Computer Society, *Code of Conduct*, 22 April 1992

Personal characteristics

→ Excellent communications skills – ensure the message is understood and conveyed correctly.
→ Management skills – ensure work is completed and information handled well.
→ Analytical – able to visualise, e.g., changing design information into information systems.
→ Problem solving abilities.
→ Flexible within the role – projects have a habit of changing midway through and the ability to be pragmatic is essential.

Ethics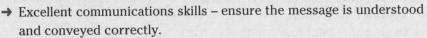

→ ICT attracts money and money has a habit of attracting unethical behaviour.
→ Codes of Practice and Conduct are set down by organisations to help professionals understand what ethical and unethical behaviours constitute.
→ British Computer Society advocates this as they see it as raising the profile of the ICT profession.
→ Some employment contracts have a code of conduct relating to ICT built in. Non-compliance leads to disciplinary action and ultimately to being sacked.

Malpractice and its effects on information systems

→ Damage the reputation of:
  → the individual.
  → the organisation.
  → the industry.
→ Loss of public confidence.
→ Creates public misconceptions, e.g., software or hardware that only operates as other, non-standard components are available.
→ Computer misuse leads to fears about viruses, etc., – extra expenditure on suitable protection software.

Examiner's secrets

The examiner will be keen to see that you understand the difference between Codes of Practice and Legal Obligation.

The jargon

Ethics – a set of algorithms for judging right and wrong in a given situation.

Checkpoint 1

Describe why it is important to be able to trust that information handlers will deal with data in an ethical manner.

Check the net

The British Computer Society has information relating to their codes of practice and codes of conduct on their web site: www.bcs.org.uk

Plugging weak points in information systems ●●●

If information about a system indicates it has bugs, etc., the professional should deal with this thoroughly, not by plugging holes.

Plugs lead to:

→ Short-term solutions – quick fixes that do not stand up to rigorous use.
→ Millennium bug situations – memory expensive – save costs by using 2-digit representation of numbers. Then ten to fifteen years later . . . the rest is history!
→ Expensive long-term fixes.

This behaviour is deemed unethical and unprofessional by the British Computer Society's Code of Conduct, element 10:

"Members shall not misrepresent or withhold information on the capabilities of products, systems or services with which they are concerned or take advantage of the lack of knowledge or inexperience of others."

Check the net

Using your favourite search engine, carry out a search on the *millennium bug* – try to find sites before and after 2000 to see any differences in reporting style.

Checkpoint 2

Why is it important for ICT professionals to be flexible in their approach to work?

Checkpoint 3

Why do 'quick-fixes' often prove counter-productive?

Exam questions   answers: page 48

1

ADVERTISEMENT

WANTED SOFTWARE ANALYST/
PROGRAMMER

REQUIRED TO WORK WITH
DEVELOPMENT TEAM.

Applicants trying to get this job need certain qualities: list *four*. (10 min)

2 'Codes of practice' and 'legal requirements' are not the same thing in the ICT industry.
Explain, with the aid of *two* examples, the distinction between a legal requirement and a code of practice.   (10 min)

3 Professional progression within the ICT industry requires more than just technical skills. Give *three* other necessary qualities and explain why they are important.   (10 min)

Examiner's secrets

Questions which suggest *two* or *three* responses will be made clear to you. Always put the right number of responses down – no more and no less!

Legal framework

As more reliance was made on ICT and systems began to increasingly hold more personal data, checks needed to be placed on the use of this data. Legal frameworks came into being for two purposes – for protection of the data subject and as a benchmark for data users.

Data Protection Act 1998

The DPA was introduced into the UK in 1984 after 20 legislation-free years for two reasons:

→ To enable the UK to participate in the transfer of personal data within the EU – Council of Europe data protection convention.
→ Public concern over data held within commerce and industry.

Eight principles apply:

→ Personal data must be obtained and processed in a fair and legal manner, i.e., with consent.
→ Personal data must be held for specified legal purposes – declared by the holder at registration.
→ Personal data must not be used for any reason incompatible with its original purpose – *can be tricky when data is sold on to a third party*.
→ Personal data must be accurate and up-to-date.
→ Personal data must be relevant and adequate – *this ties in with the previous principle*.
→ Personal data must not be kept longer than is necessary – either because the data is no longer relevant (e.g., a spent criminal conviction) or because the subject is deceased.
→ Personal data must be made available to the individual concerned and provision made for corrections – links, value and importance of information.
→ Personal data must be kept secure – this protects the subject and the holder.

Exemptions

There are some exemptions to the Act which fall into two categories:

→ Exemptions – **data**
  → Payroll, Accounts, Pensions.
  → Names and addresses held for distribution only.
  → Statistical data may not be accessed by subjects.
→ Exemptions – **access**
  Data may only be accessed by the subject unless:
  → Accessed by your legal representative, with your permission.
  → You are in mortal danger, e.g., medical records.
  → National security is threatened.
  → Prevention of crime.
  → Tax or Duty collection.

Study tip

Begin with all eight principles in longhand and try to condense them into one- or two-word statements.

Checkpoint 1

Give two reasons for the development of the DPA.

Watch out!

'Personal data' is data relating to a living person who may be identified from it, e.g., National Insurance Number – just a collection of letters and numbers but one that has a 1:1 relationship with an individual.

Examiner's secrets

Be aware of the exemptions. You may be faced with a scenario involving one or more of them.

Check the net

The Data Protection Act from the government's point of view can be seen at: www.dataprotection.gov.uk

This act covered data held by electronic means and left paper-based data with little protection and its subjects with no rights. In *October 1998*, the original act was *amended* to include the same rights of protection to paper-based records.

The Act also created the post of Data Protection Registrar (now the Information Commissioner) to act as administrator for companies registering their data and as arbitrator for individuals or *data subjects* having issue with the holders of data.

Computer Misuse Act 1990

The Computer Misuse Act (CMA) gives users clear definitions of what does and does not constitute misuse, and can be used as a basis for a civil and criminal court action. There are three criminal offences defined:

→ Unauthorised access to a computer system – hardware, software and data (this includes 'accidental' incidents).
→ Unauthorised access with intent, i.e., non-accidental access.
→ Unauthorised modification of computer materials, e.g., by virus or data manipulation.

Copyright, Designs and Patents Act 1988

→ Protects software against theft and alteration.
→ Protects the intellectual property of programmers and designers as both software and ideas are covered.
→ Organisations such as BSA (British Software Alliance) and FAST (Federation Against Software Theft) established to audit organisations' licensing of software and initiate legal proceedings if found to be unlicensed or inadequately licensed.

EU Directive on the Protection of Individuals with regard to the Processing of Personal Data and on the Free Movement of Such Data 1995

This directive mainly reinforced the UK DPA. There are a couple of differences:

→ Access to medical records may not be denied.
→ If access is denied to the subject, the directives supervising authority can check the lawfulness of the processing being applied to the withheld data.
→ National Security agencies no longer exempt from supervision.

Checkpoint 2

Explain when an individual should not have access to information about themselves.

Watch out!

Many texts were produced prior to this amendment – paper-based records *are* covered by the Act.

Checkpoint 3

Every adult has a National Insurance Number. Can this be used to identify an individual?

Check the net

The following site has interesting insights into the CMA 1990 and the Copyright (D&P) Act 1988: www.itsecurity.com

Study skill

Referring to this as the EU Directive – Protection of Individuals, Processing and Free Movement of Data will help you remember all aspects covered!

Check the net

A website dedicated to ICT law and EC perspectives can be found at: www.cla.org/eclawbook/ecl_00.htm

Exam questions   answers: pages 48–9

(a) The Computer Misuse Act has *three* levels of offence – give examples of each. (12 min)
(b) Misuse of standalone PCs whether accidental or deliberate can be reduced by the use of certain measures – suggest *four*. (15 min)

Health and safety

Check the web

An excellent site with detailed research into computer-related health problems is: www.newcastle.edu.au

Checkpoint 1

Describe how to avoid RSI when using a computer.

Check the net

British Standards Institute: www.bsi.org.uk
e-mail: info@bsi-web.com

Checkpoint 2

It is recommended that VDU users take a break regularly – why?

Test yourself

Computers are relatively safe machines to operate. However, they do give rise to discomfort in the back, eyes and hands. Look at the lighting and seating in your suite, and make a survey of problems that you and other people have had.

Computers have made many jobs much more productive. They have radically altered the way we perform our daily tasks. Many people now spend a much greater proportion of their working time actively using their computers. However, some people are finding out that these machines can cause a variety of painful health problems.

Types of health risks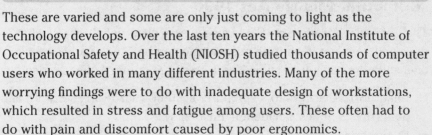

These are varied and some are only just coming to light as the technology develops. Over the last ten years the National Institute of Occupational Safety and Health (NIOSH) studied thousands of computer users who worked in many different industries. Many of the more worrying findings were to do with inadequate design of workstations, which resulted in stress and fatigue among users. These often had to do with pain and discomfort caused by poor ergonomics.

Types of risks

→ Musculoskeletal.
→ Eye fatigue.
→ Electromagnetic emissions.
→ Laser printers.
→ Lighting.
→ Ergonomics.

Musculoskeletal discomfort

Sitting for long periods of time will usually cause discomfort. It is therefore vital that the chair, desk, keyboard and so on are positioned in such a way that the operator is comfortable for the maximum amount of time. Repetitive strain injury is not a new illness but RSI is known to have links with poorly positioned keyboards.

Seating is one of the prime causes of discomfort and is linked to the back being in the 'c' position instead if the natural 's' position. A 'Beleans' chair forces the user into the correct position but are fairly scarce in the ICT industry.

Eye fatigue

This can occur if the eyes have been focusing for a long time on an object that is nearby. This has been linked to poor lighting and lack of breaks in viewing the VDU. There is at present no evidence that this type of strain will cause permanent damage. Most discomfort is caused by the operator not blinking enough, which results in the eyes failing to be refreshed.

Electromagnetic emissions

Computers do give off *minute* amounts of radiation as a by-product of their technology. The amount however falls well below the permissible amounts allowed by international radiation safety groups. The soft X-rays actually only travel a few inches away from the monitor tubes before they dissipate so are unlikely to cause harmful side-effects. *The law* – Computer manufacturers must rate each piece of equipment with a rating, which corresponds to their maximum levels of radiation. Glassware is now stringently controlled.

Laser printers

Laser printers give off ozone gas – a mild irritant – as a by-product of the electro-photographic process. This will not present a problem if the printer is set up in a well-ventilated position.

Lighting

The position of lighting and reduction of reflective light are both important considerations when positioning a computer. Because computer displays are self-lighting, users probably need less lighting rather than more. Positioning a computer in front of a window can cause glare on the screen, which causes rapid eye fatigue. Many offices now use up-lighters, which bounce soft light off the ceiling rather than shine directly at people.

Ergonomics

The best workstation is one which provides the user with the greatest comfort and safety. The key to this is to ensure the body is in a normal rather than abnormal position. Using ergonomic data the *eyes, neck, hands, wrists, arms and backs of legs* are less likely to suffer from any damage. Designers and office equipment manufacturers all use ergonomic data that is readily available. The charts give average sizes, reach, heights and so on for men, women and children of all ages.

Take note

All monitors have to have an emissions rating. Check yours out and try to put it in context, say with an X-ray unit!

Checkpoint 3

Why do manufacturers use average sizes, reach, height, etc.?

Exam questions   answers: page 49

1   Computers are here to stay but some office workers decided that their eyes were being damaged and are worried about using them.
    As the office manager how could you reassure them?   (2 min)

2   You have been given five new computers for a light and airy office with windows on two sides and walls on the other two.
    How would you position the computers so the operators work in comfort?
    (8 min)

Answers
Ethics, law and social impact

Control of information

Checkpoints

1 Recording of sales data against customer details, allowing statistical investigation.
2 Saves cost of market research, ensures independence of information, can be greater in profile than some companies may have access to.
3 Answers from: security of the individual's data, protection of individual, avoidance of misuse.
4 From: anti-terrorism, crime detection, sexual abuse of children, harassment.

Exam questions

1 There are various ways that companies could go about gathering information:
Market research – using their own research department, asking potential customers or clients.
Hiring a third party to do the research for them
There are whole industries of information specialists that could be approached. They can supply data regarding consumption, use, taste and so on by gender, age, locality, income and many other factors.
2 The main advantage that an online survey has over more traditional methods is that once the form has been designed, it runs the data gathering without human intervention. There could be hundreds of people filling in the questionnaire at a time, from all over the world. Their results are automatically harvested and stored electronically. The data can then be manipulated and presented automatically, giving running scores, or final results, literally at the touch of a button.

Value and importance of information

Checkpoints

1 Ability to target specific products to a locality, target advertising at a sector of customers, to encourage them to purchase similar items, or more expensive versions of their usual items.
2 Companies allow purchases on credit, the rating of an individual affects how much credit they can be allowed, therefore restricting what they can purchase.

Exam questions

(a) A negative effect that can come about through incorrect information being given to the specialist companies could be:
Following statistical analysis of results, the suggested patterns are not what the majority of the public believe to be accurate, for example public opinion surveys often sample 100 people, if those 100 are all from one social class, or region, they may skew the results of the survey to their, perhaps, biased opinions. It is important that the survey group is chosen carefully.
(b) Surveys such as that described above are often carried out by using written questionnaires; mistakes may be made through mis-reading the questions. There could also be errors with the data entry when the results are being prepared for analysis.
(c) Companies carrying out such surveys may try to develop a set of control answers with which to compare the results. There may also be different ways of gathering the data, using market research personnel to ask the questions, making all questionnaires multiple choice, or using a larger sample.

Capabilities and limitations of information and communications technology

Checkpoints

1 To improve and update their web presence, to ensure that they direct sales correctly.
2 Secure data can be sent across borders, is available at any time, international working such as telesales, use of cheap labour to carry out tasks.

Exam question 1

ICT systems can store unlimited knowledge from a range of human sources; thus the ICT systems' body of knowledge can be potentially greater than any individual's.
An ICT system can process the knowledge in at least two distinct ways:
• It can be structured as a database that can be interrogated by a number of structured rules.
• It can examine a vast number of combinations of input states and make comparisons with standard possibilities.
ICT systems can control multi-media delivery systems and thus present a range of stimuli and information in a context that could not be matched by a human.

Examiner's secrets

This type of question is asking about the aspects of ICT systems that allow them to outperform humans, not simply mimic them.

Exam question 2

Examples of ICT systems that would cause havoc if they failed are:

Human, for example:
Life support machine failure:
• *The patient may die.*
• *The hospital may be sued.*
Car sensory braking system failure or motorway/rail traffic signal control failure:
• *Cars or trains would crash.*

Economic, for example:
Gas billing of customers who have moved to a different supplier:
• *Causes a loss in customer confidence which may lead to a loss in profitability.*
Denver airport baggage handling system consistently failing:
• *Led to delays in opening the airport and huge financial losses.*

Environmental, for example:

Failure in tanker on-board navigation system:

- *Causes beaching and subsequent environmental damage.*

Social impact

Checkpoints

1 Individuals that have access to the Internet can take part in further education.
2 Harassment, spam e-mail, junk mail.

Exam question 1

In structured essay or paragraph format, the following points would gain you marks.

Social

- Ease of access to knowledge.
- Large body of knowledge gives in-built second opinions.
- Potential for social manipulation by suppression of selected information.
- Reduction of human interaction skills, importance of human comfort.

Moral

- Greater equality of opportunity to have access to knowledge.
- The dangers of such unlimited access without advice and human interaction.

Legal

- Possibility of extensive vetting of the stored knowledge due to the legal obligations of the providers of the system.
- Individual humans being less accountable.

Exam question 2

The types of organisation likely to advertise on such systems

- Firms with a wide distribution base such as InterFlora.
- Suppliers of specialist products, e.g., stamps, binoculars etc.
- High-street stores such as Argos.
- Obvious net-friendly products such as computer software – from a range of vendors.
- Video and CD suppliers as they have easily transportable products.
- Supermarkets for convenience shopping.

The capabilities and limitations of such systems for this activity

- Cannot try out products, e.g., test-drive car/try on clothes.
- No physical queue except for the speed of graphic download from slow servers or your modem.
- Limitations in browsing tools may make some sites difficult to access.
- Sales pitch offer an integration of text, sound and video, e.g., hotel/holiday bookings.
- Limitation in products offered – sometimes not the full range available in store.
- Some suppliers have limited knowledge of their system and may fail to deliver if unable to view your purchases.
- Retailer can collect statistical information on customer habits.

The potential security risks for the customers in using such a system

- No central controlling body.
- Different laws exist in different countries – purchases made on the net of products illegal in this country mean you will not be able to receive the product, even after paying for it, e.g., telecommunications devices.
- Not all suppliers use secure servers, therefore, small chance of hackers obtaining your credit-card details.

The organisational impact of such systems

- Reach a wider market, no longer dependent on geographical site.
- Less susceptible to 'local factors', e.g., strikes, weather.
- Changes in working practices and organisational structures.
- Costs of equipment/paying site designers and maintainers.
- More prone to hacking/false advertising.
- Reduction in prime-site office costs.
- Reduction in service costs.
- Fewer employees.

The social impact of such systems

- Psychological factors.
- Less people to meet.
- Buy more because it is available.
- Buy less because the impulse to buy is not there.
- More pleasant to shop away from the crowds/queues etc.
- Can shop from home.
- More flexible shopping hours.
- Reduction in city centre and transport usage.
- More environmentally friendly.
- Create cities devoid of people.

- Could increase equality of opportunity.
- Opportunities for those with physical disabilities.

Exam question 3

Problems and solutions that disabled people might have using the new word-processing package:

Trouble differentiating colours causing eye strain	Change colour configuration
Difficulty using mouse	Change the sensitivity or the speed of operation
Difficulty using keyboard	Slow down auto repeat

Information and the professional

Checkpoints

1 Without trust, information is withheld, that means decisions based on the information may be incorrect.
2 Technology is continually evolving, to keep up, the professional needs to retrain constantly.
3 Trying to rectify a fault, without careful research and development of the solution, can make the solution fail therefore making the original problem even worse, and this in turn, lowers public confidence.

Exam question 1

The following is a list of qualities that would benefit an analyst programmer:

- Ability to work as part of a team – can exchange views, share information, fit in with normal software/hardware development teams.
- Good oral communication skills – enables efficient and effective communication with users, aids interviewing and questioning.
- Good written communication skills – able to write documentation that appeals to technical and non-technical end-users.
- Organisation/line management skills – able to take and give orders, can take responsibility for their own work and delegate when necessary.
- Ability to listen – an inability leads to misinterpretation of end-user's needs and wants.
- Perseverance/problem solving – both analysis and programming are careers that require the ability to stick at problems and see them through.
- Ability to tease out end-user requirements.
- Communication skills – generally.
- Adaptability and ability to take on new skills.
- Logical, reasoning skills.
- Able to work under pressure and meet deadlines.
- Willingness to professionally develop – via training and as a result of criticism.

Exam question 2

Legal requirement – data protection
Legal requirements regarding the need to respond to queries about data are specified within the act, while a code of practice may highlight an acceptable timescale that a response must be made in.
Code of practice – hardware/software sales
Any legal requirements are subject to the Trades Description Act. However, a professional code of practice may prohibit a salesperson from selling hardware/software that they know is soon to become obsolete.

Exam question 3

Refer to the answer to question 1.

Legal framework

Checkpoints

1 Enabling sharing of data across European borders. Public concern over the storage and use of data by companies.
2 Legal representative gains access in your stead. Mortal danger. Threat to National Security. Prevention of crime. Tax or duty collection.
3 Yes, it has a 1:1 correlation.

Exam questions

(a) Level 1 – *unauthorised access* to material *without any intent* to do anything other than just gain access. An example would be the student who gains access to the administrative side of a college network or to another student user. The person who tries to get into a system just for the hell of it.
Level 2 – *unauthorised access with intent to commit* or to facilitate commission of further offences. For example accessing bank records with the intent of committing fraud. Accessing personal details with the intent of committing blackmail.
Level 3 – *unauthorised modification* of computer material. The code or data is actually changed rather than simply viewed and used. For example changing the balance in a bank account, altering someone's credit status, changing an examination mark.
(b) The following is a list of acceptable replies:
- Password protection to prevent access to software by third persons.

- Keyboard locks to prevent physical use of the equipment.
- Isolation of machine in a locked room with restricted access to it.
- Automatic virus check – software permanently installed.
- Automatic backup to prevent data being inadvertently lost.
- Screen savers – to prevent unauthorised viewing of data.
- Automatic shut-down if no action is taken within a pre-defined period.
- Read/write restrictions on certain files to prevent changes being made to important data.
- Vetting of employees.
- Training.
- Procedures/code of practice/employee contract – forced recognition.
- Authenticity of software – purchased from a reliable source.
- Encryption of data.
- Audit trail.
- Removable hard disk.
- Shutting down the system correctly.
- Saving to floppy and removing from the premises.

Health and safety

Checkpoints

1 Careful positioning of mouse/keyboard/VDU to avoid strain. Use of appropriate seating and other furniture.
2 To avoid eye strain from the screen, to stretch muscles, therefore avoiding other muscular strains, improve concentration.
3 Average sizes will meet the needs of a large proportion of the population.

Exam question 1

There is no evidence that monitors damage the eyes permanently, but operators should rest regularly and work in an environment that does not make viewing the screen difficult.

Exam question 2

Facing an open window can cause glare, any reflection should be reduced to a minimum. Seating and desk should be purchased for their ergonomic qualities and equipment positioned accordingly.

Revision checklist
Ethics, law and social impact

By the end of this chapter you should be able to:

1 Understand how information has become a commodity of most businesses.	Confident	Not confident **Revise** page 32
2 Describe how information subjects can gain access to information held about them.	Confident	Not confident **Revise** page 33
3 Know what the term 'lifestyle information' means.	Confident	Not confident **Revise** page 34
4 Have a comprehension of the effect of information that is incorrect.	Confident	Not confident **Revise** pages 34 and 35
5 Recall the main characteristics of quality information.	Confident	Not confident **Revise** page 36
6 Offer a succinct definition for the term MIS – Management Information System.	Confident	Not confident **Revise** page 36
7 List the benefits that ICT-based systems have over non-ICT based systems.	Confident	Not confident **Revise** page 37
8 Know what the 'information society' is.	Confident	Not confident **Revise** page 38
9 Recall the effects that ICT has had on employment patterns.	Confident	Not confident **Revise** page 38
10 Offer a list of benefits to people with special needs.	Confident	Not confident **Revise** page 39
11 Tell the difference between a code of practice and legal obligation.	Confident	Not confident **Revise** page 40
12 State the names of the major acts of law concerning ICT and data.	Confident	Not confident **Revise** pages 42 and 43
13 Offer scenarios where the CMA 1990 can be invoked.	Confident	Not confident **Revise** page 43
14 Discuss the eight principles and exemptions relating to the DPA 1998.	Confident	Not confident **Revise** page 42
15 List some common health risks linked to ICT.	Confident	Not confident **Revise** page 44

Data – capture, organisation and management

Data that is carefully captured, organised and managed will provide an organisation with invaluable information. This information in turn will lead to the generation of knowledge that will help the organisation to flourish. Data capture techniques and the verification and validation of captured data, need to be carefully monitored to ensure that high-quality data-input exists. As various organisations need systems for different purposes, so different modes of processing exist, to help them tailor their system to their purpose. How data is distributed and disseminated will also reflect on the organisation. Many systems exist to act as a holding centre for data that is subject to periodic recall. Various techniques exist to help maintain effective control over data, ensuring that it retains integrity, while also providing an effective management tool.

Exam themes

→ Definitions of knowledge, information and data

→ Appropriate methods of data capture

→ Definitions of validation and verification

→ Appropriate use of validation techniques

→ Application of processing modes

→ Creating effective database structures

→ Synopsis of the role of DBMS and their administration

Topic checklist

○ AS ● A2	OCR	EDEXCEL	AQA
Data, information and knowledge	○		○●
Data capture	○		○
Validation and verification	○		○
Manipulation and processing	○		○
Dissemination and distribution of data			○
Data types and basic representation	○	○●	○
File types	○	○●	
Database design	○●	○●	○●
Databases – analysis and design	○●	○●	○●
Database design – normalisation 1	○●	○●	○●
Database design – normalisation 2	○●	○●	○●

Data, information and knowledge

In order to be useful, a computer must have *input* to *process* and convert to *output*. These three functions of a system have certain parallels in data, information and knowledge.

Data

→ Raw facts.
→ Has no intrinsic meaning.
→ Is unorganised.
→ Is not understandable.

Information

→ After processing, has meaning.
→ Is organised.
→ Is understandable.
→ Contains facts directly relevant to the data collection event.

Knowledge

→ Information in context.
→ Permits inference – filling in the blanks.
→ Aids decision-making.
→ If – then – else.

By putting into a paradigm the relationship that a teacher has with the progress of a student, we can see the development of data, information and knowledge.

Checkpoint 1

Describe the difference between data and information.

The jargon

Inference – reasoning an answer based on prior knowledge.

Take note

Data, information and knowledge are not interchangeable concepts. Organisational success and failure can often depend on knowing which of them you need, which you have and what you can and can't do with each.

Take note

There's a clear difference between data, information and knowledge. Information is about taking data and putting it into a meaningful pattern. Knowledge is the ability to use that information.

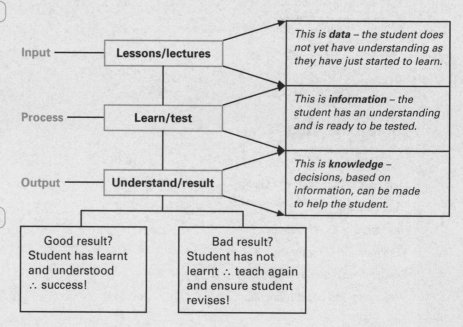

Coding and encoding ●●●

As the use of technology has permeated society, the amount of data being stored, manipulated and transported has increased dramatically.

This has led to a growth of systems that code data to ensure that only certain users can access it. This often incorporates some method of compression.

An early form, used before computer systems is shorthand – this is a method used by reporters to record a conversation in a written form. Normal writing is not quick enough to record at the speed that people speak, so a system of squiggles and marks was developed. Anyone trained in the use of shorthand could decipher the marks and reproduce the text of the conversation.

Data can be held in a shorthand format – some advantages and disadvantages of this are:

Advantages	Disadvantages
Saves space	Loses meaning
Hides sensitive data	Loses precision
Speeds data entry	Quantifies the qualitative – e.g., value judgements

There can be conversion errors; however, there are many checks put in place to try to avoid this happening. Control data is often used to ensure that entries are validated.

Links

Sections on the Value and importance of information (page 34), and the Capabilities and limitations of ICT (page 36), hold more data relating to this topic.

Checkpoint 2

What is the use of information in context?

Checkpoint 3

Why are computers so useful in the acquisition of knowledge?

Exam questions   answers: page 74

1   Many market research firms use questionnaires as a means of gathering raw data for companies about the popularity of their products.
    (a) Explain why information technology is widely used in market research.
    (b) Once the data has been collected, it can be used to give the clients information about the company's products. Explain the difference between information and data in this context.   (12 min)
2   Information encoded about value judgements as data can have the effect of reducing its accuracy or meaning. This becomes evident when the data is retrieved and used. Explain, with the use of two appropriate examples, why this may happen.   (8 min)

Data capture

The purpose of the captured data will have an effect on the method chosen to capture it. In almost all situations, a combination of methods will be used in order to get the best quality data possible.

Take note

Make notes on the items below in **bold**.

Techniques

Organisations often employ specialist companies to gather data and then encode it and enter it into the database or manipulation system. These companies often employ a variety of methods, and have specialist trained staff carrying out the operations.

Direct

→ Could be as a **result of an action**, e.g., log-on times to a network is data that could be collated into information for the network manager to use as evidence for future node procurement.
→ Via **observation** – a technique used commonly in systems analysis as the analyst is not reliant on what users *think* happens, but by watching the event themselves.
→ **Questionnaire** – if these are well written, they can form the basis of sound data capture. The data will be in an easily managed format as long as sections for comment have not been included.
→ **Work study** – the documentation of features of an old system which can be quantified and applied to the relative cost/benefits of a new system. Data received would be compared to predictions for the new system – can easily be affected by opinion, e.g., the users want a new system, no matter what, so the old system is slated and its strengths overlooked.
→ **Interview** – particularly important when gathering data for the basis of knowledge-based systems. Many experts are unable to voice exactly why they know 'XYZ', so an interview would be used to let them talk through the events that occur, prior to decisions being made and the interviewer puts these chunks into words.

Checkpoint 1

Describe the term 'data capture'.

Each of these require interaction with the object of the information collection – usually the prospective customer.

Indirect

Data may occur as a by-product of data collected for another purpose. For example: data collected via questionnaire on spending habits for a supermarket may give the local NHS Trust details of the dietary habits of the local population.

Examiner's secrets

In a systems analysis scenario you could be asked to describe why one direct data capture technique is better than another. The examiner expects you to be able to form a good argument.

Sources of data

The organisation needing the data needs to work out where the data should come from:

Internal to the collector, e.g., by observing processes:

The security gate of a factory could supply data relating to the most common times of arrival – operatives clock on 15 minutes later – studying what goes on in these 15 minutes may lead to better use of resources – maybe their lockers are placed too far away from the clock machines.

External:

→ Bought-in – using a third party to gather the data.
→ Media – TV or radio requests.
→ Trade events – conferences.
→ Government statistics – nationwide surveys.
→ Demographics – localised information.
→ Internet – web questionnaires.

Data capture devices

Various systems have been developed to aid with data capture. Some of these involve automating the processes, e.g. OCR (optical character recognition), whereas others are used in supporting the work of the collectors; the use of set questions in a telesales system.

Checkpoint 2

Why should sections for comment be avoided in a questionnaire used for data capture?

Checkpoint 3

Explain why a computer monitoring system could be more accurate than a manual system.

Links

See Input and output devices (page 8). The techniques and sources of data discussed here have associated hardware with which to capture the data for input.

Checkpoint 4

How does the surge of electricity use help work out which programmes the public are watching on TV?

Examiner's secrets

Make sure you read all parts of a question before you tackle it – look at this question – the reply to part (a) commits you to part (b) – make sure you can talk about each chosen method in depth.

Exam questions   answers: page 74

The nature, quantity and quality of data often dictates the method by which it must be captured for use within an ICT system.

(a) Name *four* different methods of data capture.

(b) For each method:

(i) Give examples of the type of data which may be captured;

(ii) State the reason why this method is particularly appropriate.   (20 min)

Validation and verification

In order for information to be truly valuable to an organisation, we must ensure that the base data input is in its most correct form.

Take note

Make a card with the various validation techniques on them – think of two or more occasions where you might use each method.

Checkpoint 1

Why is it important to check data transmission?

Watch out!

Validation does not exist to check the *accuracy* of the data – it merely checks that it is *sensible*.

Checkpoint 2

Internet sites often ask for a password. Once entered they often ask for it to be entered a second time – why?

Validation techniques

Transcription or transposition errors are easily made. In order to minimise and ultimately eliminate their occurrence, various techniques have been developed to ensure that entered data is as valid or as sensible as it can be.

→ **Range check.** The input data must fall between at least two boundaries. For a Club 18–30 holiday where the holidaymaker's age falls between the ages of 18 and 30.

→ **Check digit.** Allocation of an extra digit to a product code that is calculated from the product code itself, e.g., ISBN. The digit has no meaning of its own.

→ **Hash total.** Items may be assigned a hash value. All hash values will be added together at the end of the process and if they equal the amount they should, the operator can see they have included all items for the process. The number has no meaning outside the context of being used to validate data input.

→ **Control or batch total.** This is also used to double check that all items have been included in a process but this number will have meaning. This is a handy technique used for checking till balances at the end of the day.

→ **Format check – picture check – input mask.** Input data must follow a certain standard, for example the majority of UK postcodes follow the format:

Letter, Letter, Number, Possible Number, Space, Number, Letter, Letter. Of course exceptions exist so flexiblity must be maintained.

→ **Look-up check.** The use of certain data to trigger a search for other data. For example postcode and house number when used by call centres usually provides the operator with the full address. This can be a useful security feature for telephone banking.

→ **Presence check.** Requiring that data is input to a field. This is a technique that can be seen on many e-mail forms – they usually require the user to provide an e-mail address or various other details, or the form is not processed.

→ **Data type check.** This is automatic validation. If a system has been pre-set to accept a date field and text is entered, it will be rejected as it does not match the data type.

Transmission checks

Data corruption can occur during transmission and due to the volume and importance of data being transmitted electronically, there are some validation techniques reserved for transmission.

→ **Parity.** The parity bit is added to every byte that is transmitted.
→ **Checksum.** The numeric value of the bytes in a block of 256 will be used to generate a result and the result will be transmitted with the data. When received, the same calculation will be performed and the two numbers compared; if they do not match, the data is re-sent until they do.

Integrity

These checks are used when matching records from transaction files with master files:

→ **New records** – checked to ensure they are totally unique.
→ **Deleted records** – checks the file actually exists before the record is deleted.
→ **Consistency** – ensures that new data is not going to disrupt the system by providing conflicting data.

Verification

Verification is the process where the computer seeks confirmation from the user about the correctness of the data entered. It may take the form of entering the data twice to ensure it is correct. It is commonly used in batch systems, where two or more clerks enter the data and keep doing so until it is the same for both clerks and can also be seen when you set up a password.

Check the net

You'll find excellent definitions of many ICT terms at: www.webopedia.com

The jargon

Parity – The quality of being either odd or even.

Example

The parity bit for each byte is set so that all bytes have either an odd number or an even number of set bits. As the transmitting device sends data, it counts the number of set bits in each group of seven bits. If the number of set bits is even, it sets the parity bit to 0; if the number of set bits is odd, it sets the parity bit to 1. In this way, every byte has an even number of set bits. On the receiving side, the device checks each byte to make sure that it has an even number of set bits. If it finds an odd number of set bits, the receiver knows there was an error during transmission.

Action point

Using a relational database that you are familiar with as an example, write down how you would use each of the validation checks highlighted – do the same for a spreadsheet you are familiar with.

Exam questions   answers: pages 74–5

1   A school uses an information system to store details of students' examination entries and results. As part of this system a program is used to check the validity of data such as candidate number, candidate names and the subjects entered.

   (a) Suggest *three* possible validation tests which might be carried out on this data.

   (b) Explain, with an example, why data which is found to be valid by this program may still need to be verified.   (10 min)

2   Distinguish clearly between a check digit and a parity bit.   (5 min)

3   Describe the difference between data verification and data validation.

(3 min)

Manipulation and processing

Every system will have been designed with its processing purpose in mind. Data is manipulated in a certain manner to fulfil this purpose. Data is also manipulated and processed according to its type.

Batch processing ●●●

This requires the preparation of all relevant data for a process prior to the process being run. This mode can be applied to data that is input by a variety of methods.

→ A single user inputting all the data. For example a payroll clerk in a small business.
→ Many users inputting the data over a time period. Monthly credit control – producing balances.
→ Via automatic data transfer – quarterly billing in a utility organisation – gas, telephone etc.

In order to avoid a bottleneck at the end of the processing period, many organisations have a separate department to input data offline, as it arrives – this is called key-to-disk – the data is then processed in a batch at a later time, without the need for human intervention.

Transaction processing ●●●

If the user requires confirmation of the results of processing then they need to use a system that will allow for this feedback. Transaction processing follows a process through from start to end.

→ Generally used in commercial systems.
→ Allows for instant feedback, e.g., booking a cinema ticket and paying for it on your debit card could provide you with actual tickets and a debit on your account balance, all within a couple of minutes. Stock checking systems used in high street catalogue stores that alter as transactions occur.
→ Can help to reduce error. If a transaction needs to be completed before the sales system can commence another transaction, double booking *should* be eliminated.

Another name for transaction processing is pseudo-real time.

Interactive processing ●●●

This system involves the user interacting with a computer, responding to immediate feedback. Sometimes the system acts in a similar way to transaction processing with processes being carried out to completion, for example:

→ A booking with a travel company involves the use of various computer systems culminating in the reservation of an actual seat on an actual aircraft.

At other times, the system takes on the characteristics of batch processing for example:

"The operational or processing mode is the way a computer system is used and operated."

British Computer Society, *Glossary of computing terms*, edn 8, 1996

Checkpoint 1

'Real-time' processing must have the ability for human interaction – why?

Take note

Make a list of other instances of batch processing.

Checkpoint 2

Bank statements are often batch processed – why?

Examiner's secrets

The examiner will be impressed by good use of the terminology backed up with clear examples of use.

Checkpoint 3

Credit-card fraud may be halted by the use of transaction processing, but many stores use interactive or batch processing. What is the advantage to the store?

Check the net

Many organisations have online shops where you can browse, reserve and pay for goods in one transaction.

→ The purchase of clothing in a shop for which payment is made on a debit card – the transaction with the store system is complete, but the store may save up all of their debit transactions and process them in a batch, overnight after the operator has interacted with the system in order to send the data.

Real-time processing ●●●

BCS: '. . . *real-time system is one which can react fast enough to influence behaviour in the outside world'*.

→ On-line system with instant access
→ May or may not be interactive – for example the real-time thermostat systems employed in nuclear reactors that raise and lower the rods as they cool in order to prevent meltdown, are part of a non-interactive control system
→ Need to have the possibility of human interaction, for example an air traffic control system that cannot be overridden would be as unsafe as using no tracking system at all.

Processing different types of data ●●●

Text is stored in strings or a series of strings. It is then either processed as a string or it is manipulated to fit a purpose. Its main uses are as a method of representing language for output or as a search medium. Text strings are used to initiate searches on the www for example, or can be concatenated to produce meaningful output.

Graphics come in two forms – raster and vector.

→ *Rasters* are pixel-based, bit maps and are large to store, as all sections are 'recorded'. Quality is dependent on the screen resolution.
→ *Vectors* are based on complex mathematical equations and are smaller to store as only the co-ordinates from the equation are stored. They are employed frequently in CAD and graphic design.

Sound – this type of data has many uses. The most common is in the production of music, where analogue samples are taken and manipulated to create new, digital sounds. This data can then be produced easily for distribution on CD, MP3 or other formats. Digitised sound has the ability to emulate the human voice and be output as voice synthesis, helping those previously unable to communicate through speech to do so.

Take note

Create your own definitions of the various modes of processing.

The jargon

An analogue to digital converter is needed to produce sound that is in a binary form and can therefore be stored.

Examiner's secrets

Remember to address all parts in a multi-part question.

Exam questions answers: page 75

1 Why is transaction processing known as pseudo real-time? Does this cause a problem? (4 min)
2 Giving reasons, explain which mode of processing you would apply to each of the following:
   (a) School attendance register.
   (b) Selling tickets for an event using a call centre.
   (c) A piloting system for docking passenger ferries. (15 min)

Dissemination and distribution of data

Having changed your data into information, you probably need to get it to an audience. There are many different methods for doing this – each suited to a slightly different occasion.

Output formats

All information is only useful when it is communicated to others. It is important that an organisation thinks very carefully about the method used to present its information to others, particularly if the information is to be shown to people outside the organisation.

→ Textual – e.g., printed reports, press releases.
→ Numeric – e.g., reports.
→ Graphical – e.g., presentation of slide shows, posters. Charts or graphs.
→ Audio – e.g., multi-media report, telephone, video conferencing or a presentation.
→ Motion – e.g., robotic reaction to a procedure.

Whichever output format is chosen, the producer must be aware of the audience. This does not mean 'dumbing down' or intellectualising the content. It simply means that the message will convey the appropriate meaning no matter who the recipient is.

Types of report

There are various types of report that an organisation may, in an appropriate manner, use. Some of these are used at specific points in a project, or at set times.

→ Operational report – a snapshot of the situation for a given time.
→ Summary report – groups of data usually detailing information for a set amount of time – day, week, etc.
→ Exception report – a summary of the summary – a report that only highlights new data or items that need action, for example, if something is out-of-scope, over-budget or has missed a deadline.

Reports are important documents and a lot of care is taken to make sure that the correct report is used at the correct time. Errors made in reports can jeopardise whole projects.

Checkpoint 1

What would be the most appropriate output format for a music sample?

Checkpoint 2

Would an exception report be written every week?

Don't forget!

Your coursework submissions may well make use of reports and it would be a good idea to ensure they have these characteristics.

Desirable characteristics of reports ●●●

Desirable characteristics are:

→ **Relevant** – in content and context to your audience.
→ **Complete** – may lead to bad decisions if incomplete data is used as the basis for your strategy.
→ **Accurate** – again to safeguard against bad decisions.
→ **Clear** – unlike the message presented to a group of factory workers in South Wales who were given a presentation on the company's expansion into Europe and how fantastic it was. It wasn't until the next day that people realised they had been made redundant *en masse*. Their company was actually relocating.
→ **Timely** – reports need to be delivered on time and contain detail that is up to the minute.
→ **Concise** – should only contain relevant detail, e.g., an exception report.
→ **Logical** – should follow presentational conventions regarding layout.

Report generators ●●●

These are software tools developed to make report generation more straightforward by:

→ Creating professional looking reports
→ Using your spreadsheet or database data as the content
→ Not requiring the user to be a programmer
→ Automatically updating when new data is made available
→ Having the ability to add on functional data, e.g., via queries using structural query language (SQL)
→ Saving time on production meaning up-to-the-minute data and reports can exist.

Checkpoint 3

Why is accuracy important in a report?

Checkpoint 4

How can report generators help to produce a logical report?

Exam questions   answers: pages 75–6

1   The head of a sales team has developed a presentation. It is planned for members of the sales team to deliver this presentation as part of a sales talk to large audiences at various locations throughout the country.

    (a) State *three* advantages to be gained by using presentation software as opposed to the use of traditional methods, e.g. OHP.

    (b) State *three* design considerations that should be taken into account when the heads of the sales team are developing the presentation.

                                                                    (8 min)

2   List briefly the functions of a report.   (2 min)

Data types and basic representation

Data type information set by the programmer will not only help humans to understand the meaning of items in the system, it will also help translation of the code and the smooth execution of the program.

There are many types of data – some are language dependent, others as a result of programmer preference. The following is a list of the most common types in use but is not intended to be exhaustive:

Character

These are singular symbols and can take the form of letters, digits, punctuation marks, spaces and even non-printing control characters, e.g., CRLF symbols which inform the printer to carriage-return, line feed, etc.

They are stored as binary integers which in turn refer to the character set held by the computer set held by the computer – some examples of these sets are EBCDIC (Extended Binary Coded Decimal Interchange Code), ASCII (American Standard Code for Information Interchange) and ANSI (American National Standards Institute).

String

This is formed by making sequences of characters, e.g., your name, postcode or even your telephone number, as long as you bracket the dialling code.

Strings are variable in length by nature but can be fixed and have certain characters restricted if so desired, e.g., file names in pre-long file name capability, where the maximum eight digits for use were restricted in both length and the type of characters held (no spaces, etc.).

Numeric

There are two types of numeric data:

→ **Integer** – any whole number, negative, zero or positive.
→ **Real** – number that makes use of fractional parts, i.e., a decimal point.
  Two variations of real:
  ⇒ Fixed point notation.
  ⇒ Floating point notation – uses standard form to express the position of the decimal point.

Checkpoint 1

Defining the type of data is essential – why?

Take note

Make short notes on each of these data types. Then, using your practical knowledge, make notes stating why you chose to employ each of these types when developing your own software.

Watch out!

Using a string data type for a telephone number field shows good design thought – why would you assign a number field as you will never need to perform a calculation on it?
Setting it as a text field will make it more flexible and easier to manipulate, e.g., ( ) around codes, EXT to denote an extension line on a switchboard, EXDIR to indicate it is ex-directory and must not be publicised.

Watch out!

Zero does not exist as a normalised floating-point number. Instead the smallest positive number closest to zero is used.

You are not expected to perform these calculations but should be aware of the implications of their use.

→ Integers are not complex – process more quickly.
→ Real numbers take up more storage space but are more precise.

Boolean ●●●

→ Has one of two values – 0/1, on/off, true/false.
→ Can represent logic.
→ Commonly used to minimise program size as booleans are small.
→ Can help to control program flow.
→ Are used by the ALU to perform binary arithmetic.

Byte ●●●

→ A group of bits that represent a character.
→ A data type used to represent a small number.
→ A group of bits that represent an instruction or memory address.

Special data types – data and currency ●●●

→ Data will be in a form that can be predicted or always follow the same format.
→ Will perform basic validation, e.g., £150.037 would be queried, because two digits only would be expected after the decimal point.
→ Can allow for conversion, e.g., input via a keypad = 1.12.90, output on the VDU = 1 December 1990.
→ In their basic form, they are small to store – 'add-ons' may make them less efficient, e.g., currency fields that display negative amounts in different colours.

Checkpoint 2

Why have systems like ASCII come into being?

Checkpoint 3

What is an integer?

Test yourself

In a credit control system, why would the data type *date* be more efficient than a *string*.

Checkpoint 4

Is there a limit to the length of a string of data?

Exam questions answers: page 76

1 Give examples of simple data types – explain in simple terms. (4 min)
2 Two aspects of data types are poorly understood – explain the difference between data type and its representation. (6 min)

File types

Just as data comes in different formats or types, so do files and the manner in which they are stored. Different techniques exist for files held for different purposes.

Serial

Records are stored one after another and may only be recalled in this same order.

→ *For example* – imagine you have a diary that does not contain an alphabetically pre-set address section. On meeting new people, you simply add their details to your list. In order to extract a telephone number, you will need to read down your list, from top to bottom, going through each person's record until you discover the data required.

→ *Where would they be used?* – ideally suited to applications where data can be held in this serial manner until they have a sort or extraction process run against all of them, e.g., storing the results from a questionnaire – it doesn't matter what order they are in as you are only interested in the totals – not each individual record.

→ *Advantages and disadvantages* – a fast storage method that doesn't wait for hardware to catch up with you as it records data in the next available space. Ideal for use with magnetic tape storage or disk media.

Sequential

Records are stored in an order determined by the sort performed on it, e.g., ascending numeric order for client account numbers.

→ *How does it work?* – the field within the record that the sort was based on becomes known as the key field.

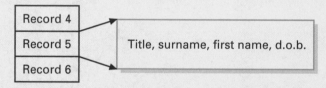

A sort in alphabetical order by surname would result in this:

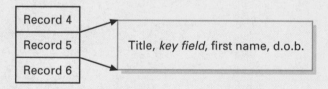

→ Accessing the correct record is similar to serial access – each record is read until the correct one is found – easier to identify than serial as there is some order due to the key field. To equate this to the diary example, imagine you have been able to organise your friends into alphabetical order but still on the same page.

→ *Advantages and disadvantages*
  → Can be slower than serial if writing changes to the master file as the correct line must be located before changes are made and recorded.
  → Popular when used for batch processing.
  → Ideal for use with magnetic tape storage media or disk.

Checkpoint 1

Describe one advantage for using the serial method of recording data files.

Take note

You need to make notes about each of these file types so that questions asking you to suggest backup solutions, for example, can be confidently handled.

Checkpoint 2

What form of sorting would be carried out to arrange a set of data files in reversed alphabetical order?

Indexed sequential

Fundamentally, this is an enhanced sequential filing system.

→ *Primary index file* is created which contains a subset of data, e.g., for our diary example, the subset of data would be the letters of the alphabet.

→ *How does it work?* – access is via query of the primary index file, e.g., I need to find my friend Lucy – her surname is Rees, so I access the part of my system that stores all the surnames beginning with 'R' – I then search sequentially for her details by looking for the key field – remember I have already sorted this into alphabetical order based on surname.

→ *Advantages and disadvantages* – storage media will be disk, allowing random access.

Random access

Records possess unique identity features, i.e., key field data, enabling them to be located and accessed without the need to locate or access any preceding records

→ *Where would they be used?* – especially useful for systems that require quick access and updating, e.g., a call centre for a customer service function – there is no way of knowing who is going to call next, therefore quick access to any record is essential.
A derivation of this is the non-sequential processing involved in hypertext systems – files are usually stored in a pseudo-structured manner, e.g., all in the same folder, but can be accessed in any order – this is easier to visualise if you use a frames hypertext system.

→ *Advantages and disadvantages* – magnetic tape is not a suitable media – hard and floppy disks or CD media may be used.

Binary

Binary data is stored in a similar way to random access files.

→ *How does it work?* – made up of a series of bytes, each of which can be directly addressed.
Useful for extraction of large data blocks that do not need updating, e.g., library files.

Take note

Most database programs contain four main object types: tables, queries, forms and reports.

Checkpoint 3

What is the advantage of using an index file?

Checkpoint 4

Explain why serial recording is more appropriate for tape stream systems.

Exam questions   answers: page 76

1   Sequential access data files
    The concept of using a sequential file to store invoice data by company name is very simple. Just enter the data as it is found in a filing cabinet. To access the information, begin reading at the start of the file and continue until finished. What would be the drawbacks of using this simple system?   (4 min)

2   Random access data files
    Random access data files could be considered easier to access – why is this?

                                                      (3 min)

Database design

One of the most beneficial software developments has been the database. It allows the convenient storage and retrieval of data and is being coupled with excellent presentational features, e.g., reporting and online publishing.

Take note

Make comprehensive notes on each of the **bold** items.

Characteristics of good design ●●●

Time spent at the analysis and design stages of a software development will help to produce databases that operate efficiently. Well designed systems display the following:

→ Minimal **data redundancy** – this refers to the amount of duplication in a system.
→ **Data consistency** – a result of redundancy is the occurrence of instances where one duplicated field is up to date but others are not.
→ Minimal **data/program dependence** – where changes can be made to the structure of the data without having to completely rewrite the system.
→ **Data integrity** – refers to both the security of data and its consistency during and after processing.

Examiner's secrets

You may need to describe the characteristics of good database design using real-life or possible scenarios – make sure you are prepared!

Relational v. flat file ●●●

→ Data held in a flat file is insular – any queries/processes involve the whole dataset.
→ In relational databases, tables are used to hold data specific to the table name (entity). Queries use only the data from relevant tables, e.g., a system has twelve tables and data from three is required for a query – only these three are manipulated. This makes processes faster.
→ Changes in a flat file system can be labour intensive, e.g., a client whose name appears many times changes their address – each occurrence of their address would have to be updated – granted, find and replace functions make this easier, but if a relational database was used, the one entry in one table that holds address data is all that needs to be altered.

Watch out!

Never suggest the use of a relational database where a flat file database will do the job (and vice versa).

Entities: attributes and occurences ●●●

Take note

Define each of the **bold** words – different sources call them different names – on your definition cards, state each of the 'also known as' names you can find.

Entities – items that make up the database, i.e. tables
Attributes – characteristics of these items, i.e. fields
Occurrences – details of the attributes, i.e. data

CAR			
MAKE	MODEL	ENGINE SIZE	INSURANCE GROUP
VW	Passat	1800	8
Citroën	Xsara	1400	6
Ford	Fiesta	1100	2

Conceptual models ●●●

These are theoretical models of any database. They show the entities and how (if at all) they relate to each other.

Relationships

We concern ourselves with three distinct types:

→ **One-to-one** – 1:1, e.g., one car : single owner/driver.
→ **One-to-many** – 1:∞, e.g., one car : shared drivers.
→ **Many-to-many** – ∞ : ∞, e.g., many cars : many fleet drivers.

In diagrammatic form these may look like:

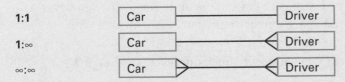

1:1 Car ——————— Driver

1:∞ Car ——————— Driver

∞:∞ Car ——————— Driver

These are known as entity relationship diagrams or ERDs.

In order to see the complete database in this diagrammatic form, many ERDs are linked together, e.g., a customer contact database which has the following entities:

Customer, organisation, order:

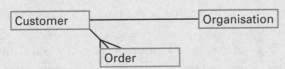

Customer —————— Organisation
        └ Order

This shows that each organisation places one individual as the customer contact and that this individual is responsible for many orders in the system.

In order to clarify why you have given certain entities certain relationships, labelling your model is advisable.

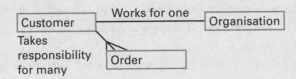

Customer — Works for one — Organisation
Takes responsibility for many — Order

To double-check your relationships, work them backwards as well, e.g., to check that the relationship between customer and order is one-to-many. Think logically – many orders belong to a customer – this is correct because if the relationship was 1:1, i.e., one order belongs to one customer, then a new file would have to be created with each order as more than one order cannot belong to a customer.

Test yourself

What might happen if this customer/order relationship was defined as many-to-many?

Exam questions   answers: pages 76–7

1 There are two main types of database: flat-file and relational. The one which is best to use for a particular job will depend on factors such as the type and the amount of data to be processed, not to mention how frequently it will be used. Discuss the advantages and disadvantages of each. (12 min)

2 What do you think makes a 'good' database? List the criteria you think should apply. (5 min)

Databases – analysis and design

Many database design techniques are double edged. They not only help you when conceiving ideas and comprehending structure but they also help others understand what you have done. Other database design techniques exist to ensure your system works as efficiently as possible.

Standard notation

This is a written convention applied when designing tables and their contents – *Use It*!

The entity is written, in the singular, in capitals outside the brackets. The primary key or composite key data is underlined. Foreign keys appear in italics and spaces in attribute names are filled in with an underscore! In other words . . .

ENTITY (<u>primary_key</u>, address_one, address_two, <u>foreign_key</u>)

Definitions of the various keys

→ **Primary key** – a unique identifier, e.g., your passport number.

→ **Composite key** – a combination of attributes that, alone, are not unique, but when combined are unique, e.g., your surname, initial and date of birth in a club database.

→ **Foreign key** – an attribute that is not part of the key in one table but is in another.

→ **Secondary key** – also known as index – formed when data is sorted into a specific order and the system creates a corresponding index that results in data retrieval being speeded up.

Data flow diagrams

Research has shown that the majority of projects fail to produce a successful system due to a lack of in-depth analysis of both the current system and the end-user's requirements. Although data flow diagrams are technically analysis tools, their use is advised in order to produce well-designed databases.

In order to document how data flows through a system to enable the capture of a snapshot of the processes involved, systems analysts developed a simple diagramatic tool. Data flow diagrams can be general and describe the system in overview, or they can be specific and go into great depth regarding minute sub-processes.

Checkpoint 1

Define the style of standard notation.

Take note

Ensure that you can clearly define each of the **bold** terms.

Checkpoint 2

Data flow can be observed in a complete system, or part or subsystem. How can this be recorded?

Data flow diagrams (DFDs) make use of four basic symbols:

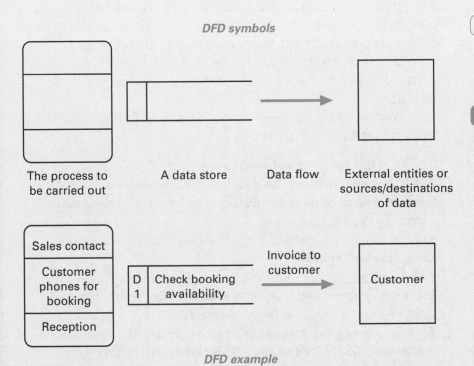

DFD symbols

The process to be carried out	A data store	Data flow	External entities or sources/destinations of data

DFD example

Watch out!

Entity in this case means an external or internal recipient or generator of data or indeed an object.

Checkpoint 3

Why should all symbols in a diagram be annotated?

There are many ways to produce a DFD that is technically correct, especially if the system being analysed is complex. That being said, there are still some rules that need to be adhered to when using DFDs.

1   Annotate everything well, i.e., process symbols, entities, data flows, etc.
2   Data must not flow straight out to an entity from a data store; a process must be undertaken first.
3   Level 0 or context DFDs involve only entities and data flows.
4   Level 1 DFDs involve all of the symbols.

Exam question   answer: page 77

What are the differences between random access data files and indexed access?   (5 min)

Database design – normalisation 1

This is a set of rules applied to data which should result in well-designed databases. Normalisation itself was proposed by a mathematician – Edgar Codd when he first experimented with relational databases.

We are concerned with the first three of the rules of normalisation and will use the following data to illustrate.

Scenario – the system is to be used for exam entry records within a school.

1 List all of the data that you need to hold.
   Entry ID, name, surname, address, town, postcode, telephone number, date of birth, exam number, subject name, date of exam, start time, board, fees, retake?

2 Choose an entity name, e.g., ENTRY and a primary key – arrange using standard notation.
   ENTRY (<u>entry ID</u>, name, surname, address, town, postcode, telephone_number, date_of_birth, exam_number, subject_name, date_of_exam, start_time, board, fees, retake?)

3 Form a table of your attributes and put in the data for a single occurrence, i.e., for one student. This clearly shows data that will repeat.

Checkpoint 1

How many rules of normalisation should concern you at this point?

Study tip

Work through this example and then apply the theory to data-handling problems of your own.

Checkpoint 2

What is an ENTITY?

Entity ID	First name	Last name	Address	Town	Postcode	Telephone number	Date of Birth
13728	Ian	Jones	3 The Hollies	Hove	HE3 4BX	01234 456789	13/12/82

Exam number	Subject name	Date of exam	Start time	Board	Fees	Retake?	
5328	IT	18/05/00	9.30	NEAB	£25		
5329	IT	16/06/00	2.00	NEAB	£25		
7218	DT	20/05/00	9.30	OCR	£18.70	Yes	
7219	DT	24/06/00	1.30	OCR	£32		

4 Identify the attributes that repeat by square bracketing them in your standard notation dataset.

ENTRY (<u>entry ID</u>, name, surname, address, town, postcode, telephone_number, date_of_birth, [exam_number, subject_name, date_of_exam, start_time, board, fees, retake?])

Data is now in its un-normalised form.

1NF – first normal form

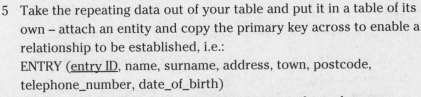

5 Take the repeating data out of your table and put it in a table of its own – attach an entity and copy the primary key across to enable a relationship to be established, i.e.:

ENTRY (<u>entry ID</u>, name, surname, address, town, postcode, telephone_number, date_of_birth)

EXAM (<u>entry ID</u>, exam_number, subject_name, date_of_exam, start_time, board, fees, retake?)

6 The chosen key is not sufficient for this table – it does not *uniquely* identify an exam that a student can take. The choice of key can be difficult and many combinations look possible.

For example – entry ID and exam_number – an OK combination as long as a student does not wish to resit (exam boards may use the same exam number for the duration of a syllabus).

Try entry ID, exam_number and date_of_exam as the composite key. This is unique as it is impossible for this data to repeat – the year part of the date_of_exam attribute will age!

7 Update your standard notation record.

ENTRY (<u>entry ID</u>, name, surname, address, town, postcode, telephone_number, date_of_birth)

EXAM (<u>entry ID</u>, <u>exam_number</u>, <u>date_of_exam</u>, subject_name, start_time, board, fees, retake?)

Your data is now in first normal form!

The jargon

1NF – first normal form . . . any attributes with repeating values are removed.

Checkpoint 3

Why is normalisation carried out?

Checkpoint 4

Why is it important to have unique primary keys?

Database design –
normalisation 2

This section needs to be read alongside the preceding one in order to give you a full appreciation of normalisation. Second and third normal form tweak the table contents so that they allow the database to perform in as straightforward a manner as possible.

Checkpoint 1

Define the term 'composite key'.

The jargon

2NF – second normal form . . . all attributes that are not part of the primary key must be dependent on the whole primary key, not just part(s) of it.

Checkpoint 2

What does the term 'query' mean?

The jargon

3NF – third normal form . . . all non-key fields must depend completely on the key field.

2NF – second normal form

8 Concentrate your attentions on any table that uses a composite key. Are all of the attributes meant to be there? Look closely at the parts of the EXAM table that do not make up part of the primary key.

EXAM (entry ID, exam_number, date_of_exam, subject_name, start_time, board, fees, retake?)
→ Subject_name is only dependent on exam_number.
→ Start_time is dependent on all parts of the key.
→ Board is only dependent on exam_number.
→ Fees are only dependent on exam_number.
→ Retake is only dependent on entry ID and exam_number.
Remove the attributes that are not dependent into separate tables where they depend on their own primary keys. In other words:

EXAM (entry ID, exam_number, date_of_exam, start_time)
EXAM_detail (exam_number, subject_name, board, fees)
RETAKE (entry ID, exam_number, retake?)

Making a note of your other, unchanged tables is necessary alongside your 2NF tables:

ENTRY (entry ID, name, surname, address, town, postcode, telephone_number, date_of_birth).

3NF – third normal form

9 You may find that moving from 1NF to 2NF has automatically sorted your tables into 3NF. In order to confirm this, you need to look very closely at all of your tables to ensure that attributes are dependent on the primary key, not simply on other attributes in the same table.

In our worked example, we see that:
→ Subject depends on exam_number.
→ Board also depends on exam_number.
→ Fees depend on the exam board and the exam_number – this means that fees have a non-key dependence that needs to be removed.

At the end of normalisation to 3NF, our tables should look like this:

ENTRY (<u>entry ID</u>, name, surname, address, town, postcode, telephone_number, date_of_birth)
EXAM (<u>entry ID</u>, <u>exam_number</u>, <u>date_of_exam</u>, start_time)
EXAM_DETAIL (<u>exam_number</u>, subject_name, <u>Board ID</u>)
FEE (<u>Board ID</u>, exam_number, fees)
RETAKE (<u>entry ID</u>, <u>exam_number</u>, retake?)
BOARD (<u>Board ID</u>, <u>exam_number</u>, board)

10 To test your normalised data, run a hypothetical query – can you extract the surname of all students taking an exam at 9.30 a.m. on a certain date if you know the board they are sitting with?

→ From the BOARD table, get exam_number.
→ From the EXAM table check exam_number against date and start_time of exam to extract entry IDs.
→ From ENTRY cross match all extracted entry IDs with surnames.

This proves that this data is normalised in an acceptable manner.

Data dictionary ●●●

This is a collection of data about the database. Data dictionaries do not have any set format but tend to be structured table-by-table, with information about the entities, primary and other keys, attributes and the properties of those attributes (see the section on data types for more information on these).

Data dictionaries are useful tools for both day-to-day running and administration of a database and for more in-depth fault-finding during maintenance.

To illustrate, here is the start of a dictionary for the ENTRY table:

ENTRY			
Attribute	**Data type**	**Validation**	**Notes**
Entry ID	Text	Pre-set format	Unique number allocated to students on entry to school. Contains text and numbers.
Name	Text	Entry required	Max 20 characters long
Surname	Text	Entry required	Max 25 characters long

Checkpoint 3

Why is a 'data dictionary' useful when maintaining a database?

Watch out!

Remember that it is possible for a set of data to be normalised by two different people and the end result to be slightly different, based on the way that the people see the relationships between tables working.

Checkpoint 4

Why would a database dictionary contain the maximum length of some data strings?

Test yourself

Continue this data dictionary for the ENTRY entity.

Answers
Data – capture, organisation and management

Data, information and knowledge

Checkpoints

1 Data is raw, information is refined and useful.
2 Knowledge.
3 Computers are very good at information handling, data storage and retrieval. They can save people time and energy in developing knowledge.

Exam question 1

(a) The speed with which data can be processed allows quick turnaround of data and, therefore, more accurate results, important as industry has to monitor consumer demand which changes quickly.
Data can be manipulated more easily thus allowing a wider use of statistical techniques, for example the use of statistical analysis software or more simply the production of graphs.
Increased accuracy meaning data collected is more useable.
- Data can be read directly from documents avoiding transposition errors.
- Pre-set options allow more accurate results.
- Calculations or averages and sums, etc., are more accurate.

Volume
- It can handle far greater volumes of raw data meaning that larger samples can be taken and more accurate results obtained as a result.

Also items from this list but only at one point each and a maximum of two points!
- Increased accuracy.
- Increased speed.
- Ability to cope with large volumes of data.
- Reduction in paperwork.
- Improved manipulation/processing/presentation of data.
- Reduced cost of operation, e.g., less survey staff required.
- Effective storage.
- Electronic data transfer – use of communications.
- Gather data at a distance.

(b) *Data* – raw facts, figures or measurements which have not been subject to processing and contain no meaning as they have no context – for example, the single questionnaire which, on its own, has no meaning.
Information – data that has been processed to give it meaning, for example the contents of all the questionnaires is processed in order to produce a graph – it is now data with meaning, i.e., information.

Exam question 2

Accuracy
- Normally a discrete coding forces coarseness, e.g., blue/green eyes must be coded as blue or green – does not allow for variations that could be interpreted differently by two individuals.

Meaningfulness
- Depends on the weight given to it by the coder of the information.

Data capture

Checkpoints

1 Collecting data electronically.
2 Too much variety in possible answers, meaning it is very difficult to generate statistical data.
3 Errors in recording avoided, accuracy against time, no need for breaks, continual observation, precision/accuracy of measurement.
4 Surges caused by use of kettles, usually in advertising breaks, or at the end of a programme – the times can be checked against the TV schedule to see what was being shown at that point.

Exam questions

(a) Observation, questionnaire, work study, interview.
(b) *Observation*: Time related reports, can be useful for planning processes, as each stage of a process can be analysed and then redefined if necessary.
Questionnaire: Short answers, useful for statistical analysis, the results can be used to justify a position.
Work study: A report detailing the processes that were being used, with guidance on how the process could be improved, and can provide detailed information, including costs and benefits.
Interview: Verbatim reports of discussion, useful for gathering data for knowledge based systems, these results are difficult to analyse statistically, but can provide a lot of detail.

Validation and verification

Checkpoints

1 Data can be corrupted by electrical or radio interference, making the result unreliable.
2 To verify that the first typed response matches the second typed response.

Exam question 1

(a) Any three from:
- A check digit applied to the candidate number.
- A lookup table of possible qualifications to check the ones claimed exist.
- A range check on the number of qualifications taken.
- Check to ensure the student name exists.
- Check result matches a subject entered.

- Presence check to ensure a result has been input when required.
- Batch totals.

(b) Validation exists to ensure that data entered is of a reasonable or sensible nature. It could well be reasonable and sensible for a student to be awarded a B grade in their GCSE ICT exam, but if that student either did not sit the exam, or indeed got a different grade, then the information that was input was both reasonable and sensible, but not correct.

A visual check, i.e., verification will help to ensure that the information is correct.

Exam question 2

A check digit is added to an input to help detect transcription errors.

Parity bits are used to help trap transmission errors.

Exam question 3

Validation is undertaken by the system – it checks the input for reasonableness. Verification is undertaken to check that base data has been transcribed correctly.

Valid data can be reasonable, yet incorrect. Data can be transcribed correctly, yet be unreasonable.

Manipulation and processing

Checkpoints

1 Over-ride, automatic systems can make decisions without the full picture, household thermostats may turn off the heating, but the user may want it extra-hot.
2 Regular output, every month, so data can be manipulated, formatted and printed in one session, without causing errors due to missing entries.
3 Processing of credit details can be done automatically, therefore employee time is not required, it can also be done over night. Saving time at the counter for customer and sales staff.

Exam question 1

Although the transaction that is being processed appears to have an instantaneous effect, there is in fact a small time-delay. This is where the term pseudo (similar to) real time comes from. This delay is as a result of the time that it takes to process data and is to be expected, so no problem is caused.

Exam question 2

(a) School attendance register
First step – define your scenario
- Daily statistics for health and safety reasons – transaction processing – as each year group or class groups' details become available then input them.
- Weekly statistics to track the attendance/non-attendance of individuals – probably on a daily basis via a batch process.
- Annual statistics for Record of Achievement purposes – again, probably using a batch process on a monthly/termly basis.

(b) Ticket sales
This is a perfect example of transaction processing – go into a little detail about the interaction of this system with the payment system.
You could mention the possibility of combining transaction processing with batch processing – collecting the payment after the tickets have been allocated.

(c) Ferry port pilot
Where human lives are involved – even with no obvious signs of danger – think real-time system. The pilot may well know the port, but what about adverse weather conditions – when they cannot judge distance as well as normal. Remember to state that the system must not be relied on too heavily and that there must be the possibility of the pilot taking control back from any guidance system they may be using.

Dissemination and distribution of data

Checkpoints

1 Audio.
2 No – exception reports are only produced when something happens that requires action – something has missed a deadline, or is over-budget.
3 Decisions are made on report data, so inaccuracy leads to misinformed decisions.
4 Generator poses a particular sequence of activities, that a user responds to. These responses are then automatically formatted into a report.

Exam question 1

(a) Three *advantages*
- Traditional output is still available, e.g., output to 35 mm slides.
- Wide range of outputs available, e.g., hard copy of individual/all slides.
- Use of video/animation to improve impact.
- Automation of presentation, i.e. do not have to physically put the OHP on to the projector.
- Provision of navigation tools.
- Ease of editing or replacing individual slides or use of templates.
- Makes the presentation 'more impressive' to the audience.
- Import from other packages.
- Remote presentations – via Internet, etc.

(b) Three *design considerations*
- Awareness of the intended audience.
- Font sizes for text.
- Quality of graphic images, i.e., distortion with size changes.
- Use of colour.
- Portability across different machines, e.g., screen resolution.
- Delivery method, e.g., video based/LCD display.
- Application of company standards, e.g., size and colouring of logos.
- Layout.
- Overloading – too much information on each slide.

Exam question 2

Reports provide a way to retrieve selected stored data and present that information effectively and meaningfully. Reports are designed to be printed out rather than viewed on a computer screen, so they need to be carefully planned. Examples of everyday reports include mailing labels, invoices, receipts, sales summaries and phone books. You can combine text, data, pictures, lines, boxes, graphs and drawings to produce exactly the report you want. Fortunately, the latest versions of the big database packages also come with several pre-planned report layouts that you can set up quickly using report wizards.

Data types and basic representation

Checkpoints

1 Computer applications can manipulate particular data types, so incorrect definition can mean that an operation will be mishandled.
2 To communicate data across the world a common language is needed, so that data can be understood and manipulated.
3 A whole number, positive or negative, or zero.
4 No – there was a limit of eight characters with no spaces or punctuation, for filenames under older operating systems.

Exam question 1

Numbers and character strings are the most basic kinds of values, simple values. A numeric value has multiple digits and a character string consists of multiple letters, but these internal structures are usually of no interest to users. The operators for these data types insulate users from the internal structure. Users can apply operators, such as comparison (=, >, <), boolean (*not, and, or*), arithmetic (+, −, *, /), or concatenate (|), to values represented as decimals or strings without having to know anything about the internal structure of values so represented. Furthermore, simple data types have generally agreed-on, well-defined representations and operators.

Exam question 2

Two aspects of data types are poorly understood. One aspect is the important distinction between the type and its *representation* – how a DBMS encodes the data type's values. This misunderstanding stems in large part from the fact that SQL's DBMS types have only one user representation, which implicitly bears the same name as the data type (e.g., the *decimal* representation of the *decimal* data type). But data types can have multiple possible representations; for example, you can represent a temperature data type as degrees Fahrenheit, degrees Celsius, degrees Kelvin, or simply hot, warm, cool.

File types

Checkpoints

1 Data can be added quickly, no need to sort and enter data at a particular point.
2 Z–A, descending order.
3 Groups data under indexed headings, enabling faster searching.
4 Tape is interrogated sequentially, from start to finish, disks can be searched randomly.

Exam question 1

With this method, the time required to find a specific record greatly increases as more and more records are added to the data file. Also, the act of adding information while trying to keep the file in alphabetical order becomes very time consuming since many existing records will have to be moved in order to make room for the new record.

Exam question 2

Random access techniques allow easier access to any particular data record. To find a data record, all that is required is the desired record number. You can then seek the proper location within the data file and retrieve the desired record.

Database design

Exam question 1

The *flat-file* style of database is ideal for small amounts of data that needs to be human readable or edited by hand.

Essentially they are made up of a set of strings in one or more files that can be parsed to get the information they store; great for storing simple lists and data values, but can get complicated when you try to replicate more complex data structures. That's not to say that it is impossible to store complex data in a flat-file database, just that doing so can be more costly in time and processing power compared to a relational database. The methods used for storing the more complex data types are also likely to render the file unreadable and un-editable to anyone looking after the database.

The *relational* databases have a much more logical structure in the way that it stores data. Tables can be used to represent real-world objects, with each field acting like an attribute. For example, a table called **books** could have the columns **title**, **author** and **ISBN**, which describe the details of each book where each row in the table is a new book.

The 'relation' comes from the fact that the tables can be linked to each other, for example the **author** of a book could be cross-referenced with the **authors** table (assuming there was one) to provide more information about the author. These kind of relations can be quite complex in nature, and would be hard to replicate in the standard flat-file format.

One major advantage is that there should be no duplication of any data, helping to maintain database integrity. This can also represent a huge saving in file size, which is important when dealing with large volumes of data. Having said that, joining large tables to each other to get the data required for a query can be quite heavy on the processor; so in some cases, particularly when data is read-only, it can be beneficial to have some duplicate data in a relational database. Relational databases also have functions 'built-in' that help them to retrieve, sort and edit the data in many different ways.

Exam question 2

With a well-designed database it is easy to enter and update information. Queries to report the information can be created quickly and relatively simply. But a poorly designed database is difficult to maintain, difficult to query, and difficult to modify.

Good database design can be summarized in three rules:
- Eliminate calculated fields.
- Eliminate repeating fields.
- Examine the relationship of non-key fields to the primary key.

The first rule of good database design is not to have any fields in a table whose value can be calculated from other fields. Another problem with this design is that it is not flexible.

Databases – analysis and design

Checkpoints

1 ENTITY (primary_key, address_one, address_two, foreign_key)
2 Data flow diagram – DFD.
3 It is essential that all readers fully understand the diagram. Symbols can be used, but they can sometimes be used for different things and to avoid confusion labels and annotation should be used.

Exam question

Random access techniques allow easier access to any particular data record. To find a data record, all that is required is the desired record number. You can then seek the proper location within the data file and retrieve the desired record.

But how do you know which record number to use? And what about adding records in the middle of the data file? How do we update or append records to our database file and still maintain a particular record order? These problems are easily solved by the use of a database management system (DBMS) such as xBase.

Database design – normalisation 1

Checkpoints

1 Three.
2 An entity is a discrete piece of data.
3 To speed up searching of a data source, and reduce file size, as each record only needs to contain data which is unique to that record, common data is stored and accessed from a second, or subsequent table of data.
4 Any duplication of keys will mean that data retrieval could return more than one record.

Database design – normalisation 2

Checkpoints

1 A key made up from different attributes in a data table.
2 Questioning a data source, carrying out an investigation.
3 It is relatively easy to check that the correct type of data has been stored against the field names.
4 So that data validation rules can be checked.

Revision checklist
Data – capture, organisation and management

By the end of this chapter you should be able to:

1	Understand how the concepts of input, process and output correspond to the concepts, data, information and knowledge.	Confident	Not confident **Revise** page 52
2	List the advantages and disadvantages of the use of coding when capturing data.	Confident	Not confident **Revise** page 53
3	Discuss the various methods of direct data capture.	Confident	Not confident **Revise** page 54
4	Describe the various sources of data.	Confident	Not confident **Revise** page 55
5	Know the difference between validation and verification.	Confident	Not confident **Revise** pages 56 and 57
6	List a range of validation techniques.	Confident	Not confident **Revise** page 56
7	Describe, in depth, a verification technique which you have experience of.	Confident	Not confident **Revise** page 57
8	Understand how different types of data are processed.	Confident	Not confident **Revise** pages 58 and 59
9	Describe the main forms of processing used.	Confident	Not confident **Revise** pages 58 and 59
10	Understand how the correctness of data can be checked when data is transmitted electronically.	Confident	Not confident **Revise** page 57
11	List a full range of output techniques used to disseminate information.	Confident	Not confident **Revise** page 60
12	Recall the major characteristics of good reporting.	Confident	Not confident **Revise** page 61
13	Describe what a report generator is.	Confident	Not confident **Revise** page 61
14	Define the following data types – character, string, numeric, boolean.	Confident	Not confident **Revise** pages 62 and 63
15	Understand the various methods used to store files.	Confident	Not confident **Revise** pages 64 and 65
16	Recall the four characteristics of good database design.	Confident	Not confident **Revise** page 66
17	Understand the differences between flat-file and relational databases.	Confident	Not confident **Revise** page 66
18	Define the terms – entity, attribute, occurrence.	Confident	Not confident **Revise** page 66
19	List the various degrees of relationship available.	Confident	Not confident **Revise** page 67
20	Know how to use standard notation and produce ERDs.	Confident	Not confident **Revise** page 67
21	Produce definitions for the following terms: primary, composite and foreign key.	Confident	Not confident **Revise** page 68
22	Use a level 0 and level 1 DFD to describe a simple process.	Confident	Not confident **Revise** page 69
23	Define the terms: 1NF, 2NF and 3NF.	Confident	Not confident **Revise** pages 71 and 72
24	Understand why the normalisation process is needed.	Confident	Not confident **Revise** page 71
25	Describe the purpose of a data dictionary.	Confident	Not confident **Revise** page 73

Networks and communication

The effect of networking and communications systems can be seen all around us. They make up the administration systems of supermarkets and control the use of resources in our schools. The potential for further development is massive – the Internet and e-commerce are evidence that new extensions of networking and communications technologies will be developed. ICT can be seen as the use of technology to automate traditional tasks in order to make them more efficient – it is fair to say that networking and communications technology is the mainstay of that theory as they enable more efficient working practices.

Exam themes

→ Network topologies

→ Network environments

→ The application of communications technology in information systems

→ Security and audit procedures involved in networking

→ The portability of data

→ Associated standards and protocols

→ Two approaches: client server and peer-to-peer networking

Topic checklist

○ AS ● A2	OCR	EDEXCEL	AQA
Network topologies 1	●	○	○●
Network topologies 2	●	○	○●
Network environments	●	●	●
Application of communications in information systems	●	●	●
Network security and audit	●	●	●
Portability of data	●	●	●
Standards and protocols	●	●	●
Client server and peer-to-peer networking	●	●	●

Network topologies 1

As ICT became an increasingly important aspect of corporate strategy, the correct co-ordination and use of resources became highlighted. Data and peripherals were discovered to be shareable resources and so computer networking was born.

Checkpoint 1

What is a 'node'?

Ring ●●●

All nodes in a ring network are deemed equal (one *may* be allocated to access control). Data is passed *through* each node until it reaches its target except in a token ring system where the data has a code or token attached to it, informing of its intended destination. Each node is then passed until the correct one is reached. Ring networks may have a repeater attached to each node, keeping the signals strong, thus enabling networks to be spread over large distances.

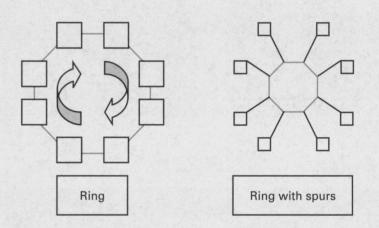

| Ring | Ring with spurs |

Advantages	Disadvantages
Transmission in one direction keeps collision to a minimum	Transmission can be disrupted if a node is down
High transmission rate	High level of access, with control difficult to implement
Not dependent on a central server	Needs a ring with spurs if it is not to be disrupted by node failure – more cable

Checkpoint 2

Why is a repeater needed in some networks, but not others?

Bus

This is the most straightforward type of **topology**. Again, no central server is required but a **node** will need a double as a PC and file or **print server**. They work best with cable lengths of less than 0.5 km and can consist of a central cable and **cable spurs** for the connection between nodes and central cable.

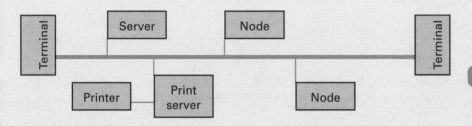

Advantages	Disadvantages
Additional nodes and peripherals easily added	Heavy usage leads to degraded signals
Least amount of cable	If the central cable is faulty, the whole network becomes inoperative
Relatively inexpensive to install	Failure on the central cable is hard to locate
Node failure does not affect the network's performance	

Take note

Make notes on all the **bold** terms.

Checkpoint 3

Define the term 'Bus' in ICT.

Watch out!

Bridge – the networks must only be the same *logical* type, not *physical* types, e.g., two LANs, one BUS and one RING could be linked if they are both peer-to-peer LANs.

Exam questions   answers: page 96

1   Give *two* differences between a local area network (LAN) and a wide area network (WAN).   (5 min)
2   Ring and star are two common network topologies.
    (i)   Explain what is meant by the term 'network topology'.
    (ii) Give *two* advantages for *each* of the ring and star topologies that are not held by the other.
    (iii) State *two* factors that affect the rate of data transfer between the computers in a network.   (12 min)

Network topologies 2

Checkpoint 1

State a reason, related to security, that would make a company use a 'star' network design for outworkers.

Star

This is a more complex topology that has a dedicated file server or hub at its centre. Data is transmitted from the server to the node or from the node to the server and back to another node, in order for data to be transmitted.

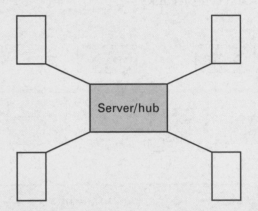

Advantages	Disadvantages
Nodes react independently of each other	Hub failure will make the whole network inoperative
Central control eases security	Hardware for the central servers is expensive
Suitable for WANs	Uses most cable
Transmission rates can be set differently for each node	May need to employ an administrator to look after the servers etc.

Checkpoint 2

Why is a 'mesh' network often used in high priority networks, such as military or security?

Mesh

This is a topology which incorporates a ring with one-to-one connections to ensure data is always transmittable. No matter which cable is damaged, nodes can communicate. The original Internet!

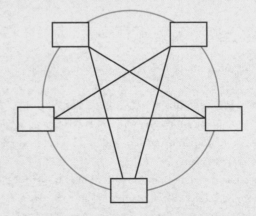

Network hardware

→ **Hub-server**
→ **NIC** – network interface card. A card attached to the motherboard that allows connectivity to the network
→ **Router** – a device that boosts transmitted signals and connects slightly different networks, e.g., a peer-to-peer to a client server that are both LANs – may be used to connect a company intranet via the Internet
→ **Bridge** – links two similar networks
→ **Brouter** – a combination of a bridge and router
→ **Repeater** – a signal booster. As signals get further away from the hub or travel a long way between nodes, they begin to degrade and require boosting
→ **Gateway** – used to connect two dissimilar networks, e.g., a LAN to a WAN over long distances
→ **Terminator** – a device used to denote the end of a cable and instruct data transmission to reverse
→ **Cable** – twisted pair, co-axial or fibre-optic – progressively more expensive, but increasingly reliable and faster.

Networks use a variety of these components to enable the software to communicate across short and long distances.

To ensure that these devices all 'handshake' or allow communication between each other there are a number of basic languages that have been developed, allowing a very low level of communication to take place. These are usually made up of a string of ones and zeros that are used to set up the connection. Once a link has been set up, the main data can be passed through the devices.

Checkpoint 3

Describe the device called a 'hub'.

Checkpoint 4

Why do networks have 'gateways'?

Exam questions

answers: pages 96–7

1 (i) Draw a diagram to show a star topology of a network, clearly labelling a file server and workstations.

(ii) In the context of computer networks, explain the purpose of each of these components:
- modem.
- switches.
- hub.
- bridge.
- router. (15 min)

2 (i) Describe or draw a bus and ring network topology.

(ii) Discuss the factors you would take into account in deciding which topology to use for a local area network. (25 min)

Network environments

Different organisations employ networked systems for different purposes, sometimes to enable sharing of resources and to promote forward-thinking, team-working practices – sometimes to obtain and maintain security. Whatever the purpose, networking should be able to offer a solution.

Local Area Networks

Key factors are:

→ They are a collection of computers linked on one site.
→ They may use cable or radio connections.
→ They ultimately exist to enable resource sharing.
→ Various topologies exist, dependent on the requirements of the end-user.
→ They can have a master/slave (client/server) relationship or an equal (peer-to-peer) relationship.

Wide Area Networks

These exist in two generally separate forms. Both use combinations of cable, radio waves, satellite transmission and communications hardware.

Private
→ Organisation-wide communication irrespective of size, time zone or location.
→ Intranets for use by one organisation or by members of one industry, e.g., Prestel as used in the travel industry.

Public
→ Global communications between all members of society.
→ Reliance on storage facilities rather than human operators – data can be accessed before, during and after office hours.

Metropolitan Area Networks

→ Used to link resources in a town/district/city to enable sharing.
→ Usually links similar institutions.
→ Tends to be non-profit-making and educational type of end-user, e.g., EaStMAN, the system that links Edinburgh and Stirling Universities.
→ Again a combination of cable, radio, microwave and satellite links will be used.

Centralised

Forerunner of commercial networks, usually a mainframe system processing data fed by dumb terminals. End-user had no control over their system and became disillusioned. The dumb terminals tended to be of a very similar type, so organisations would become locked into purchase and maintenance deals.

Distributed

These systems were developed to find common ground between the extremes of centralised processing and dispersed processing (the

Watch out!

Buildings located on one site but not physically connected can still be networked using a LAN.

Checkpoint 1

What does the abbreviation LAN stand for?

Check the net

www.eastman.net.uk
will take you to the home page of EaStMAN – the Metropolitan Area Network that links Edinburgh and Stirling Universities.

Take note

You will need a selection of real-life examples of each of these systems.

end-users making choices about platform and method of processing). It involves the linking of computers at remote sites, using desktop computers that will allow for local processing.

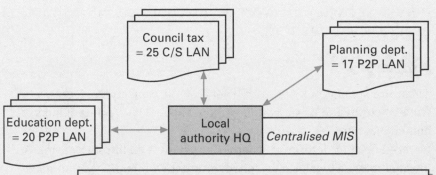

Functions carried out at different locations, with the ability to communicate and therefore control centrally.

Checkpoint 2

What is a 'dumb terminal'?

The most common system to be distributed is the database, and large national companies employ this, e.g., nationals with regional offices will hold a database that is identical to the central database except by volume, as only customers who live within the region will have data held on them locally.

There are advantages and disadvantages to this method:

Advantages	Disadvantages
Response times to queries are faster as the local database is not as large as the central one	The distributed system may not be used or administered in the same manner as a centralised system, i.e., different standards
Dependence on the central database is lessened	Relies heavily on excellent and dependable communication system
Regional offices give the customer the impression of care – local problems dealt with by local people	Security issues when distributed data is uploaded to central system

The central database is referred to throughout, as it is rare for an organisation to rely on the regional distributed systems and not amalgamate to a master for security purposes.

Exam questions   answers: page 97

1   A company has offices in six cities across the UK. Each office has a LAN. Explain *three* potential benefits that would accrue from connecting these six LANs together.   (5 min)
2   WhyZ is a company that has been very successful and is about to embark on an ambitious expansion to additional sites both in the UK and in other countries. The current location will become the company's headquarters.
    It is envisaged that the extended company will utilise distributed databases where possible.
    (i)   Outline *two* advantages of a distributed database over a centralised database.
    (ii) Describe *two* methods of ensuring data security in a distributed database and comment on the effectiveness of each.   (10 min)

Applications of communications in

Networking provides the hardware platform for organisations to utilise the capabilities of communications. The potential of networks and communications can be hinted at by the growth of Internet use but cannot be accurately measured.

Checkpoint 1

What is an encrypted tunnel?

Check the net

The Internet is not controlled by any one agency, but there are standards that have been set by some organisations that are seen as important for all serious websites. Visit: www.w3c.com to see the latest set of guidelines.

Intranets

These are simulations of the Internet on an organisational level. Data will be held by the organisation without the need for external links and communication.

Size does not determine whether a system is an intranet or not. An intranet may be local, e.g., a school intranet with copies of templates commonly used, the syllabus, even the curriculum intended by the teachers for study purposes. Different users' needs will be considered.

At the other end of the spectrum, an intranet could be global, e.g., IBM, an American organisation, uses a call centre and data processing centre in Ireland 'overnight'. Due to time-zone differences, when the company's US employees are not at work, their Irish counterparts are. This makes it appear that a twenty-four hour service is operating, without the company having to pay enhanced rates for work undertaken during unsociable hours. This system uses what is known as an encrypted tunnel.

Industry-wide intranets

Like-minded organisations amalgamate data to enhance their competitive advantage. Key points in the development of these industry-wide intranets are:

→ They started in the travel industry, e.g., Prestel
→ EDI extended the traditional definition of an industry, e.g., the consumables industry is a combination of supermarkets and suppliers who will use EDI to speed up reaction to demand
→ They provide evidence of ICT driving corporate policy and strategy
→ They also raise security issues and illustrate the need for extensive encryption/decryption systems to be in place.

Limited resources

Communications can be used to:

→ Share information, e.g., a Sixth Form project in a school set up a training intranet for the Princess Royal Hospital, Telford, where nursing and medical staff can gain access to learning materials, tests, etc., when they have the time. This would enable learning to proceed at a pace suitable to them, and fit in with the busy schedule of an intensive care department.
→ Reduce pollution – although fossil fuels are still used to produce the electricity needed to send and receive data, think of the savings made in paper, motor fuel, toxic emissions etc.

Jargon

Be careful to use the capital 'I' when describing the Internet – the world wide web. A lower case 'i' is a part of the Internet.

information systems

→ Impart knowledge to a wider audience.
→ Reduce training costs to organisations. Instructional videos, documents etc., can be stored online for access whenever required and bypass the need for a human instructor.

Exploratory work ●●●

The benefits of communications on a non-commercial level also need to be discussed.

→ Communications can allow for the remote control of experiments, e.g., measurement of climatic changes in inaccessible regions such as the Arctic – mapping of the solar system from positions other than terrestrial.
→ Potentially dangerous situations – e.g., seismic activity, nuclear reaction etc. – can be monitored using communications technologies.
→ Pioneering medical techniques can be carried out remotely or may be recorded/transmitted live to large audiences, thus enabling learning without the need for travel.

Checkpoint 2

State one difference between an intranet and the Internet.

Exam questions   answers: pages 97–8

1 (a) A company wishes to install an intranet throughout its business.
       (i)   Define the term intranet.
       (ii) Managers are able to access the intranet from home. Discuss the effect this has on the working patterns of a manager in this company.
   (b) The company provides video-conferencing facilities through its intranet. Discuss the impact this has on the effectiveness of meetings within the company.   (18 min)

2 An international company wants to set up a new computer network. Although many staff use standalone desktop systems the company has no experience of networking. As an IT consultant you have been asked to prepare a report for the company directors, outlining the issues and the potential benefits, to communications and productivity that such a network could bring. You report should include:
   • A description of the various network components which would be involved.
   • A description of the relative merits of different types of network which could be considered.
   • A description of the security and accounting issues involved.
   • An explanation of networked applications which could improve communications and productivity within the company.   (40 min)

3 A manager has upgraded his desktop computer to take advantage of his company network environment.
   State *two* changes that you would expect him to see as a result of such an upgrade.   (3 min)

Network security and audit

The use of networks for more and more core operations within commerce leads to increased security risks. The threats may come from inside or outside the organisation.

Checkpoint 1

Why is there a different version of the operating system for network systems?

Network operating systems

On top of all the 'normal' functions of an operating system, the network operating system (NOS) needs to:

→ Offer a specialised O/S with enhanced functionality.
→ Enable the sharing of resources across a network that may be accessed and utilised by many users.
→ Co-ordinate the operation and addresses of each network interface card (NIC) and the flow of data through the NIC.
→ Detect and avoid collision of data.

Checkpoint 2

Why would a network administrator need more rights and privileges than other users of a network?

The network administrator

This individual (or small team) will be responsible for:

→ Access rights and profiles, i.e., passwords and correct network usage.
→ Ensuring the hardware is compatible with the sharing of data.
→ Utilities, e.g., network virus checkers.
→ Maintenance of the network version of software – backup ensuring they do not become corrupted, etc.
→ The monitoring of usage to ensure priorities are appropriate for a given situation, e.g., traffic = heavy, therefore do not install the new virus software.
→ Maintenance and implementation of disaster recovery plan.
→ Software licensing issues.

Watch out!

Most people's passwords are members of the family, or pet names. When choosing a password for a system, try to use a selection of letters and numbers that you will remember, but will be difficult for somebody else to guess.

Need to audit internal use

→ There is a legal requirement to audit ICT systems – doing it as part of daily ICT life makes it easier to satisfy the needs of this external audit.
→ To protect the system from misuse.
→ To protect the users of the system from false accusation of misuse etc.
→ Knowledge is power – the administrator can react to problems.

Firewalls and gateways

Firewalls are software security methods applied to the gateway (hardware) when interfacing a LAN with a WAN. Firewalls can either block traffic or permit traffic to and from a gateway.

They may be used to limit the nature of sites viewed as web pages, for example, blocking out access to pornographic sites.

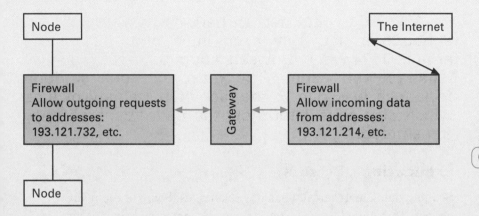

This might be the type of firewall attached to a school intranet prior to allowing access to the Internet.

→ They are used to check against virus and the nature of data being accessed, e.g., cyber patrol, Elron, Net Nanny.
→ They are not 100 per cent secure so many organisations opt for a proxy server where information already sourced and checked can be stored and manually checked at a later date. There are some disadvantages to this approach:
  → Search results are contrived – you can only find what has been filtered for you.
  → The person writing the data to proxy needs to know what they are doing.
  → Can turn into an expensive resource – hard disk space is needed if data is kept permanently.

Check the net

There are various sites on the Internet that offer firewall software. One of the most popular is www.zonealarm.com. This offers a free version of the software that can be used to protect a personal computer. There may also be software 'switches' in the operating system that can be switched on to provide some security from invasion.

Exam questions   answers: page 98

1 Explain the function of a gateway when used with local and wide area networks.   (3 min)
2 A company provides a connection to the Internet from its intranet. The security of e-mails on the intranet is maintained by the use of firewalls and encryption.
   (i) Define the term 'firewall'.
   (ii) Define the term 'encryption'.   (6 min)

Portability of data

In 1999 the Internet turned thirty-years-of-age, although it had only been in common use since around 1994 when browsers could be used to display data as web pages. The reason it took so long to launch was due to the lack of portability of data which also considered how the data appeared once transmitted.

Reduction of errors

Sending data electronically has its advantages. Some of the main aspects that have been improved through electronic transmission include:

→ Transcription errors are reduced.
→ More accurate management decisions can be made.
→ Heightens the value of information.
→ Transmission errors can be spotted and corrected more easily than transcription errors.

As data is generally more accurate when sent electronically, it speeds up the process of transmission. The transmission is fast anyway – electronic data travels at speeds approaching the speed of light, and as it is likely to be accurate it also saves time that would have been used to check the data after transmission using other means.

Dissimilar platforms

Freedom of choice and human individuality inevitably led to the design and production of items that fit the individual's ideals as perfect. Computing hardware is no exception to this and over time various different 'platforms' evolved.

The Internet prompted research and the production of products that would allow for the portability of data irrespective of the hardware hosting it.

Increased portability allows for:

→ Hardware configuration which should not determine the information and data that can be processed.
→ More choice when resourcing, e.g., networks that allow for add-ons rather than scrapping of older machines.
→ Global communications irrespective of a culture's choice.
→ Simplified expansion into new global markets. An organisation using PCs can move into a country where non-PC architecture is favoured and incorporate the hardware leading to:
  → Quick set-up and establishment in the new market.
  → A happier workforce, as at least their tools of work have not altered although their organisation may have.

The development of web browsers has enabled many of the advantages of portable data to be realised. Whereas they were designed to show

Links

See Validation and verification pages 56–7.

Checkpoint 1

What is a 'transcription' error and why are these reduced through electronic data transfer methods?

Watch out!

Java and JavaScript are different.
Java = compiled to fit needs of executing machine.
JavaScript = interpreted at runtime to fit needs of browser.

web pages, they can now incorporate additional components, plug-ins or add-ons, that allow users to view many other data types: word-processed documents, spreadsheets, multi-media presentations, even high-quality television and audio.

Java and JavaScript ●●●

In order to speed up data portability, new languages have been developed. Java is the most popular and flexible of these.

→ A portable high-level language that can run on any type of microprocessor.
→ Hardware and operating system independent as it does not interface directly with hardware.
→ Can be standalone and compiled to fit the requirements of the hardware it's compiled on.
→ Can be added to web pages in the form of applets.

JavaScript is different from Java and can be incorporated with HTML to add functionality to web pages when browsed.

Desirability ●●●

Both organisations and individuals have benefited from the improvements in the portability of data:

→ All users can communicate.
→ Global culture.
→ Hardware can be more experimental as language is not a barrier.
→ Increase in consumer choice.
→ Increase efficiency in work, e.g., teams separated by distance, working on the same projects.
→ Transferred data often had formatting applied and subsequently lost due to interpretation – this can make the whole exercise of transmitting worthless – truly portable data would not lose its formatting.

There are further improvements being made all the time.

Example

Modern web-browsing software has been adapted to enable users to watch webcast television, either on desktop machines, laptops or even PDAs.

Checkpoint 2

State one advantage of a cross platform language, such as Java.

Exam questions answers: page 98

1   'The rise of de facto standards due to commercial sales success can only benefit organisations and individuals.' Discuss this statement.
    Particular attention should be given to:
    • Operating systems.
    • Portability of data between applications.
    • Portability of data between different computer systems.   (25 min)
2   Modems are commonly used for data transmission. Explain why modems might be required.   (4 min)

Standards and protocols

In order for data to be transmitted, received and assimilated, a set of parameters needs to exist that define the acceptable hardware and software used for communication.

The need for standards and protocol

→ Different manufacturers needed to produce hardware that used standard interfaces in order to connect equipment.
→ Integration of hardware and software.
→ Global standards required as products are shipped all around the world.
→ Allow portability of data.

Checkpoint 1

Why is it important for a peripheral manufacturer to work to international standards?

OSI model

The Interactional Standards Organisation devised a seven-layer paradigm or model which clearly defines what needs to be available to each level of data communication. The Open Systems Interconnection (OSI) model was born.

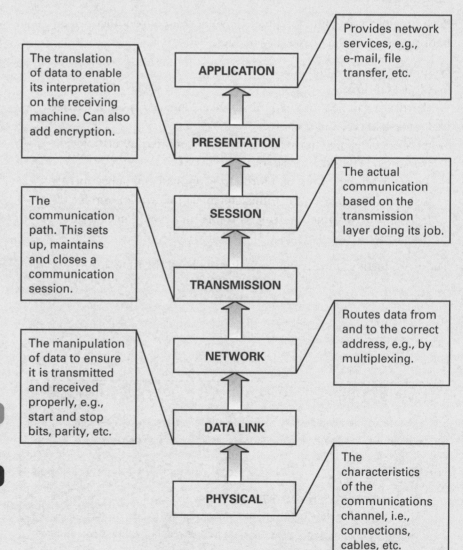

The translation of data to enable its interpretation on the receiving machine. Can also add encryption.

APPLICATION — Provides network services, e.g., e-mail, file transfer, etc.

PRESENTATION

The communication path. This sets up, maintains and closes a communication session.

SESSION — The actual communication based on the transmission layer doing its job.

TRANSMISSION

The manipulation of data to ensure it is transmitted and received properly, e.g., start and stop bits, parity, etc.

NETWORK — Routes data from and to the correct address, e.g., by multiplexing.

DATA LINK

PHYSICAL — The characteristics of the communications channel, i.e., connections, cables, etc.

Checkpoint 2

Define the term 'multiplex data'.

Examiner's secrets

You may be faced with an ethical question about reliance on the Internet. Form your reasoning well and face both sides of the argument.

TCP/IP

These are two very important protocols used when connecting to the Internet.

→ **TCP** = Transmission control protocol.
→ **IP** = Internet protocol.

The LAN *in situ* already has the correct protocols for data transmission within its system but needs assistance when communicating outside the LAN.

→ TCP can support many different connections over a network, e.g., use of the www, telnet and SMTP at the same time by many users.
→ IP ensures that data is routed correctly.
→ Both TCP and IP can multiplex data.

The jargon

To combine multiple signals for transmission over a single line or media. They can be *analogue* or *digital*.

The jargon

SMTP – simple mail transfer protocol; the protocol of e-mail services.

Internet

The global network of hardware that allows for the consultation of and collation of data. It has no owners and, as it is a global concern, does not fall under the jurisdiction of any one country. The content of the net is, however, subject to various laws in various countries. It can be used for many things, including:

* Viewing web pages.
* E-mail.
* Video conferencing.
* Remote access and control of both data and hardware.
* Data collection, i.e., informatics.

Checkpoint 3

What is a USB connection and why is it so useful?

Exam questions   answers: pages 98–9

1   A newsagent is part of a national company that runs 500 shops. Ts local
    server is connected to a computer network at the company's head office.
    At the end of the day, sales data is transferred electronically to the head
    office computer. The network also provides an electronic mail (e-mail)
    system between the head office and the shops.
    Explain the need for protocols in establishing the link between the shop
    and head office.   (8 min)

2   An ICT consultant wrote in a trade journal:
    *'The growth in technologies such as personal computers, the "world
    wide web" and "wide-area networks" has only come about because
    manufacturers and suppliers of network hardware and software have
    adopted standard communications protocols. The OSI seven-layer model
    has been a key factor in this development . . .'*
    Discuss the above statement. Particular attention should be given to:
    * The meaning of 'communications protocols' and why they are required.
    * The OSI model and a description of the role of *three* of its layers.
    * The benefits and limitations of standards.
    * Illustrate your answer with specific examples.   (30 min)

Client server and peer-to-peer networking

As different organisations use networks for different purposes, so the nature of authority and the relationship that exists between the users and the system will also be different. In order to obtain the best system for your needs, a close look at two diametrically opposed systems is advisable.

Checkpoint 1

Why is central backup an advantage for a client server system?

Client server

A network system that defines clients and servers and therefore authority. Clients are the users of data, i.e., the workstations and servers are the resource items of file servers, printers, scanners, etc.

This type of system must be managed. Somebody has to make decisions about what access rights are to be distributed to accounts across the network. These rights also have to be managed throughout the lifetime of the account.

Advantages and disadvantages of the client server (CS) approach:

Advantages	Disadvantages
Security and backup are done centrally	Limited end-user control
Resources are centrally managed	Expensive to set up
Hardware may be from different manufacturers (as long as the correct network software has been chosen)	Choice of networking software may affect the performance of applications software
Access is controlled by a network administrator	Choice of networking software may affect the hardware choices available
	Central computer reliance. If it goes down, no network processing occurs

These advantages and disadvantages need to be weighed up before embarking upon the planning of the network.

Peer-to-peer

A collection of machines, usually ten or less, that have equal authority – no single machine controls the others. Most suited for teamwork or projects.

This looser network arrangement is used to share files and information in a much less formal way.

Examiner's secrets

You may be faced with a question comparing the two systems – like-for-like. You will have a much firmer argument if you know both the good and bad points of both systems rather than simply how they compare.

Advantages and disadvantages of peer-to-peer approach:

Advantages	Disadvantages
Enable close teamwork	The machine that hosts the shared software needs to be on
Share software easily	Can be slow
Projects can be added to by many users without their being physically present	Security not great
Inexpensive to purchase	Restricted to a small number of users
Not reliant on one central computer	Quality of backup is dependent on the user
Improved morale – users are given responsibility	Each machine has the communications software installed on it, and must be individually maintained

This system should not be used where secure data is to be used.

Many large company networks employ both systems. The main corporate network is carefully managed with many users, clients, with data and account details held centrally on a server. The network is managed and maintained from a central point, and all use is monitored. However, individual departments may have peer-to-peer systems to allow for sharing of resources and ideas or collaborative working.

Checkpoint 2

Limited end-user control can be seen as a disadvantage for a client-server system, but the network administrator may see this as an advantage – why?

Checkpoint 3

Explain why many networks start off as peer-to-peer systems.

Exam questions answers: page 99

1 A company has a computer network system.
   An ICT consultant has suggested that the company changes from a peer-to-peer network to a server-based one. Give *six* features of these network environments which contrast the two different approaches.   (10 min)
2 At the central office of a landscape gardening company there are six employees. Each employee has a standalone computer system and printer. The company director has commissioned a business survey which indicated that it would be more efficient if the six PCs were formed into a peer-to-peer network.
   (i) State *three* benefits that the company would gain from networking their computer system as a peer-to-peer system rather that a server-based system.
   (ii) What additional hardware would be needed to connect the six standalone computer systems as a peer-to-peer network system? State why each item is required.   (15 min)

Answers
Networks and communication

Network topologies 1

Checkpoints

1 A junction point, where a signal is manipulated.
2 Repeaters boost the signal strength, so networks over small distances do not need them.
3 A method of transporting data through a system.

Exam question 1

A local area network and wide area network differ by:
- Geographical extent.
- The connections they use – a LAN generally uses physical connections, i.e. cable and a WAN does not.
- A LAN will be restricted to a single site whereas a WAN can be comprised of networks on many sites.
- Connections for a LAN are hardwired and transmission follows a predetermined route – WANs can use a combination of cable, modem, satellite links, etc., to route transmission in the most convenient way at any given time.
- Use of a WAN is open to many, e.g., Internet, whereas use of a LAN is by invitation.

Exam question 2

(i) Definition – a network topology is the way in which the elements of a network are interconnected (physical layout) that determines the cabling and interfaces needed.

(ii) Characteristics of a star network topology:
- Each computer is independent of the others – the system is unaffected if one computer or connection fails.
- Data transmission speeds may vary on each cabling link.
- There is centralised control of message switching.
- The central server enables good quality security.
- Easy to add new stations without disrupting the whole network.
  Characteristics of a ring network topology:
- There is less dependence on a single central computer.
- Routing is very simple – a packet will circle the ring until it reaches its destination.
- Very high transmission rates are possible.

(iii) Factors that may affect transmission across a network:
- Physical capacity of the cables.
- Protocol limitations.
- Hardware limitations, e.g., the NICs used, modem, etc.
- Difference between analogue and digital.
- Loading of the network.

Network topologies 2

Checkpoints

1 If one machine fails, the rest of the machines can still communicate and information can be re-routed.
2 Workers have to log on to a central server, therefore passwords and communication systems are easily monitored.
3 A 'hub' is the device used to bring network points together.
4 Gateways are points where network connections can leave the main network to connect with other networks.

Exam question 1

(i) Star topology of a network:

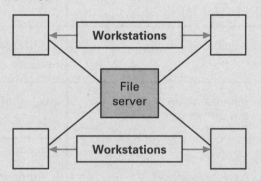

(ii) Modem – a device used to connect digital computers to analogue telephone systems.
Switches – automatic devices used for routing signals to the appropriate hub.
Hub – the point at which the single cable from the server is split so that signals can be sent to many workstations – can also be used to represent the server.
Bridge – a device used to connect two LANs.
Router – a device used to connect a LAN to a WAN or ISDN.

Exam question 2

(i)

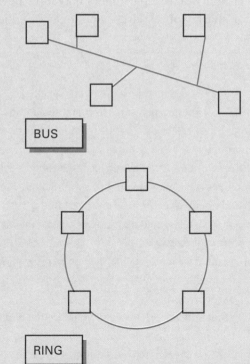

(ii) A short report discussing the following items:
BUS
- Data can be sent in both directions therefore making it slower than a ring.
- Easier to extend the network as only a single cable is needed for each new station.
- Useful where the network cannot be fully planned in advance because of:
  The need for future expansion
  Where stations are widely dispersed.
- Vulnerable to cable faults.

RING
- Enables faster communication.
- Must be planned in advance.
- More secure.
- If one station goes down the remainder are still in operation.

Network environments

Checkpoints

1 Local area network.
2 A computer, linked to a network, that has little processing power of its own, it relies on the server.

Exam question 1

Some potential benefits would be:
- The ability to share data.
- Work could be undertaken at any site – convenient for travelling sales executives.
- Each site will have up-to-date data.

Exam question 2

(i) Advantages of distributed processing over centralised:
- There is no need for a single, heavily resourced central location.
- It can provide a speedier response to enquiries which are processed locally.

(ii) Data security methods and their effectiveness:
Data encryption: Data is encoded using a special transformation key before being transmitted. It is very effective because only someone knowing the key can decode it.
Use of passwords: Access to sensitive data is restricted to users keying in an appropriate password. Users tend to be careless selecting passwords or keeping them secret so it may not be very effective.

Application of communications in information systems

Checkpoints

1 A communication system, that allows massive amounts of data to be transported over large distances, in a secure, encrypted, format.
2 Intranet is within an organisation, Internet is open to anybody with appropriate equipment.

Exam question 1

(a) **(i)** Intranet – a LAN with web-like features.
    (ii) home working – flexibility of hours, no travelling, social disadvantages, difficulty in separating home and work life.
(b) Effect of video conferencing:
    Meetings could be held at short notice.
    Can involve more staff.
    No time is lost through travel.

Exam question 2

Description of network components involved:
- Network cards in workstations to allow connection to cables.
- Routers to link network segments together.
- Switches.
- Bridges.
- Repeaters.
- Types of network cable (thin Ethernet, Cat5, ATM, fibre optic, ISDN, etc.).
- Servers.
- Gateway.
- Hub.

The relative merits of different types of networks which could be considered:
- LAN or WAN – contrast.
- Different topologies exist (give a list of types, e.g., bus, ring, star, peer-to-peer, etc.).
- Relative merits of the listed topologies (illustrate this with a discussion of the good and bad points of each topology).
- Need for routers, repeaters, bridges, etc.

The security and accounting issues involved:
- Need for hierarchical password system.
- Different types of access can be allocated.
- Accounting: recording/tracking which users are logged on etc. – audit trails.
- Accounting: recording/tracking use of systems resources.
- Need for organisational code of conduct.

Networked applications which could improve communications and productivity within the company:
- Explanation of e-mail.
- Explanation of workgroups.
- Explanation of intranet.
- Explanation of Internet.
- Distributed databases.
- Exposure to hacking – use of a firewall to limit the effect.
- Spread of virus, increased risk of exposure.
- Client/server.
- Electronic data interchange (EDI).
- Video conferencing, with an explanation of its use.
- Real-time stock control.
- EFTPOS.

Exam question 3

Changes that the manager would expect to see could include any *two* of the following:

- Additional dialogue to deal with log-in, ID and password.
- Network drives become visible in desktop applications.
- Networked resources such as printers become available in desktop applications.
- Icon/menu option for e-mail appears.
- Icon/menu option of newsgroups appears.
- Icon/menu option for browser tools appears.
- Other computers visible in peer-to-peer networks.
- Icon/menu option for networked software/applications.

Network security and audit

Checkpoints

1 Standalone users do not need the applications, so it would just slow their machines down.
2 They need to be able to delete users and change configuration. If anybody could do this it would soon become chaotic.

Exam question 1

Allows access to an external computer system in order to access a service, for example e-mail or an information system such as a database.

Exam question 2

(i) Firewall – a server that filters incoming messages to protect an internal network from viruses or hacking, etc.
(ii) Encryption – encoding transmitted data messages and decoding them when received.

Portability of data

Checkpoints

1 Rewriting, or inputting data can mean that mistakes with data entry are made. Electronic transfer means that data is only inputted once, therefore only one set of mistakes can be made.
2 Same information can be used on a range of different machines and O/Ss.

Exam question 1

Operating system
  Issue:
  Windows 95/98 has become the de facto standard for PCs, just as UNIX has become synonymous with quality mainframes.
  Benefits or disadvantages:
  Windows' 95/98 success greatly increased the fortunes of Microsoft.
  Users have benefited by having a much wider range of support services.

Wide product sales lead to international use – therefore compatibility.
Portability of data between applications
  Issue:
  Applications programming interface (API)
  Object linking and embedding (OLE)
  Benefits or disadvantages:
  Produce a set of standards which allows organisations to generate software that interfaces with other software.
  Ease of use for the individual as data can now be used in differing packages with transparency of the technical issues, for example linking data in Office or SmartSuite.
Portability of data between different computer systems
  Issue:
  TCP/IPs development as a de facto standard.
  Benefits or disadvantages:
  Organisations whose communication protocols are based on the OSI standard.
  Individuals have gained wider access to information held on differing computer systems through the Internet.

Exam question 2

- Data stored on a computer system is usually digital.
- Some data links between systems are via analogue telephone systems.
- Modems perform the translation between digital and analogue so that data can be transmitted and received.

Standards and protocols

Checkpoints

1 Goods sold all over the world, peripherals need to connect to other equipment, to maximise use, they need to connect to more equipment.
2 The ability to send and receive data to and from a number of clients.
3 Universal serial bus – a uniform connection used by various peripherals, allowing different manufacturers to work with one standard fitting and data transfer system.

Exam question 1

To ensure that the sending and receiving computers interpret the data in the same way, e.g., binary transfer and use common data transfer settings, e.g., the same number of stop bits, etc.

Exam question 2

Explanation of protocols and why they are required
  Protocols are sets of rules/conventions, defining how systems communicate with each other.

Their remit covers: cable, transmission modes, speed of transmission, data format, error detection, error correction, web addresses.

They allow any equipment using the same protocol to be connected.

Explanation of the OSI seven-layer model

Three from the following:

Application layer

- Closest to the user/highest level.
- It deals with the interface between end-users, applications programs and devices.
- Deals with accounting.
- Controls entry.
- Administers user IDs.
- FTP, HTTP.

Presentation layer

- Ensures data in different formats can be exchanged – ASCII and EBCDIC.
- Deals with encryption.

Session layer

- Users interface with the network.
- Deals with user requests for network services.

Transport layer

- Deals with data transmission between host computers.
- Administers addressing.
- Error control.

Network layer

- Routing of information around the network.
- Network accounting.

Data link layer

- Physical transmission media and any associated transmission errors.
- Deals with techniques for acknowledgement and receipt of data.

Physical layer

- Lowest level.
- Deals with mechanical and electronic connections of devices, e.g., pin connections on plugs and sockets, signal voltage levels, timings, etc.

Benefits and limitations of standards

- The need for an international forum to agree standards.
- Wider marketplace for products complying with the standards.
- Potential of standards to slow developments – waiting for standards to change to accommodate new developments.
- Ability of major manufacturers to dictate global standards, i.e. de facto standards.
- Easier to exchange files between different platforms.

Client server and peer-to-peer networking

Checkpoints

1 Easier to administer, as all data is kept centrally, a single backup can be made, from a central machine, rather than having to backup a variety of machines.

2 End-users may make changes that could damage the network. Removing their ability to do so makes the administration easier.

3 Inexpensive as each machine is similar, and there is no need for a server, or other expensive network machines. Low level of software required, most O/S have simple network software.

Exam question 1

- A reliable central computer or server exists in a server-based system – not in a peer-to-peer.
- Shared data, applications, etc., are stored on a central server rather than on any local hard drive.
- Maintenance benefit of installing once on a server, compared with installing the same software on each local drive in a peer-to-peer system.
- Increased overheads in a server system – network manager/administration staff who are required to set up and maintain user accounts.
- Shared resources, e.g., printer, hard drive, etc., only available when:
    The host workstation is on – peer-to-peer.
    The network is functioning correctly – server.
- Server-based systems can simplify the job of the network administrator – there is a reduction in network performance in exchange.
- Server-based systems introduce the single point of failure issue – i.e., no network activity = no work!
- Server implies one more capable (and more expensive!) machine that serves many clients.
- Server-based systems tend to be of a much larger scale than peer-to-peer networks.
- Software upgrades can be easy to administer on server systems.
- Security issues are harder to control on peer-to-peer systems.
- Server-based systems are likely to require additional hardware, e.g., routers, bridges, repeaters, switches, etc.
- Backup can be centrally managed on a server-based system – peer-to-peer relies on the users.
- The number of users will affect the performance of a server-based network – peer-to-peer is affected by the fact that nets of over 10 tend to be impractical.

Exam question 2

(i) Data can be shared.
    Data transfer is improved.
    Team working is more effective.
    Communications are enhanced.

(ii) Reduced cost, i.e., no purchase costs for a server.
    Reduced network management overheads.
    Network interface cards to enable connectivity and thus data transfer within the new system.
    Data transmission media or cabling also to enable connectivity.

Revision checklist
Networks and communication

By the end of this chapter you should be able to:

1	Explain in detail the different types of networks.	Confident	Not confident **Revise** pages 80–83
2	Explain the difference between an intranet and the Internet.	Confident	Not confident **Revise** page 86
3	Understand the term network operating systems.	Confident	Not confident **Revise** page 88
4	Explain why it is important to have a network security audit.	Confident	Not confident **Revise** page 88
5	Understand the roles of the network administrator.	Confident	Not confident **Revise** page 88
6	Explain why we use firewalls and gateways.	Confident	Not confident **Revise** pages 88 and 89
7	Explain the term dissimilar platforms and why they exist.	Confident	Not confident **Revise** pages 90 and 91
8	Understand what Java and JavaScript are.	Confident	Not confident **Revise** page 91
9	Explain why we need standards and protocol.	Confident	Not confident **Revise** page 92
10	Sketch the OSI model.	Confident	Not confident **Revise** page 92
11	Explain the term TCP.	Confident	Not confident **Revise** page 93
12	Explain the terms client server and peer-to-peer networking.	Confident	Not confident **Revise** pages 94 and 95
13	Sketch a range of network topologies.	Confident	Not confident **Revise** pages 80–83

The efficient and effective management of any ICT system that is in place is paramount. This stretches from the effectiveness and efficiency of any staff who may be directly involved with ICT – network manager, software support personnel, etc. – through to the use of management information systems that have been developed. This section of ICT covers many aspects from the systems lifecycle and systems analysis to corporate ICT and IS strategies.

Exam themes

→ Systems lifecycle models
→ Systems analysis and development
→ Organisational structure
→ Management information systems
→ Decision support systems
→ Executive support systems
→ Expert systems and application of artificial intelligence
→ Information flow and levels of management
→ Corporate information systems
→ Management of change
→ Audits
→ Disaster recovery
→ Legislative effects on information and communications technology
→ Project management
→ Software development
→ Policy and strategy issues

Topic checklist

○ AS ● A2	OCR	EDEXCEL	AQA
Systems lifecycle models	●	○	●
Systems analysis and development	●	○	●
Organisational structure	●		●
Management information systems	○●		●
Decision support systems and executive information systems	●		●
Expert systems and applications of artificial intelligence	○		●
Corporate information systems	○●		●
Management of change	○●	●	●
Audits	●		●
Disaster recovery	●	○	●
Legislative effects on information and communications technology	○●	●	●
Project management	●		●
Software development	●	●	●
Policy and strategy issues	●		●

Systems lifecycle models

Every system requires conception, design, building, establishing, maintenance and evaluation. The following are some models that can be applied to the development and lifecycle of ICT systems:

Checkpoint 1

Why is the process described as a cycle?

Cycle

This is a system that employs strict deadlines in its staging. The project moves in stages that must be complete prior to starting the next stage.

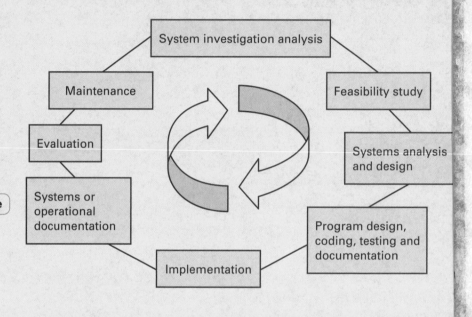

Example

PRINCE2 (PRojects IN Controlled Environments 2) is a system developed and used by various international companies and governments. It involves structuring the project in a certain way and setting up teams to work on individual parts of a project. Visit www.prince2.com to find out more.

Waterfall

A system with stages of development coupled with periodic evaluation and feedback – proactive development. Milestones are set so the system can evolve through reworking.

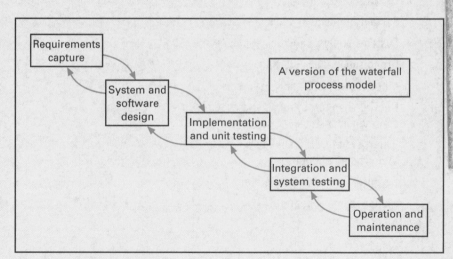

A version of the waterfall process model

Checkpoint 2

Why is it important to adhere to strict deadlines?

Spiral ●●●

Boehm's model for software development is especially sympathetic to fourth generation language (4GL) system development as prototyping is included at certain stages in development.

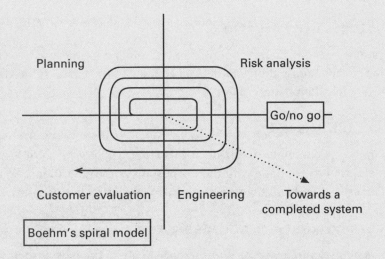

Planning

Risk analysis

Go/no go

Customer evaluation   Engineering   Towards a completed system

Boehm's spiral model

Suitability of the different models ●●●

Cycle

Either large or small projects where the development team has to complete the project in stages, or are not working in close (geographical) proximity.

Waterfall

Suited to projects involving teams – work can be done, brought together, evaluated, reworked if necessary, and subsequently signed off by the appropriate parties.

Spiral

Mainly suited to software development because a modular and prototyping approach is taken. The project grows as the team moves around the spiral.

Checkpoint 3

Which model would be most suitable for the development of software?

Exam question   answer: page 130

The waterfall model may have been used to develop a software application, such as a database. Describe in detail how the development of such a system occurs.   (40 min)

Systems analysis and development

In order to produce high-quality solutions pertaining to both hardware and software, development teams need to follow specific procedures and treat certain stages in specific ways. Many different approaches exist but most will include the following stages:

Checkpoint 1

Systems analysis can be a very expensive procedure – explain why.

Example

Microsoft Office is an enormous suite of software; the development time was measured in thousands of man years. Obviously this could not have been carried out by one man! The teams all worked concurrently over a decade, thousands of people rather than thousands of years.

Systems investigation

A systems analyst will be employed to visit and annotate any current systems. This information will be passed back to the customer in the form of a feasibility study.

Feasibility study

It is up to the customer to decide at this stage whether or not it is a viable option to continue with the proposed system alterations. Costs and projected budgets/timescales will also be factors in this study.

Systems analysis and design

This is an in-depth analysis of the requirements of the new system. Very detailed designs of the final system are produced and extensive use is made of data-flow diagrams. The flow of information is the focal point of this stage.

The documentation that accompanies this stage may include:

→ Input.
→ Processing activities employed.
→ Outputs.
→ Data models.
→ File structures.
→ Security methods employed.

Program design, coding, testing and documentation

The expertise of the programmers here takes over from that of the analysts. Programmers may be split into small teams and be allocated small sections of the system to design and code. When all has been completed, the whole system is brought together to be debugged. Documentation is a continuous process and covers every step of any project.

Implementation

The customer again becomes involved in the project at this stage. This is because they need to ensure that their office environment is ready for the new system – training, hardware, etc. The new system may be run in parallel with the old one, to ensure that it is working properly before full reliance is entrusted to it.

Systems/operational documentation

Technical manuals are produced to help with the day-to-day running of the system in its new environment.

Evaluation

The new system should be working well if all the stages have been properly adhered to. If not, the evaluation may indicate that the system has failed. In this instance, the system will be recalled from its parallel operation and be retested.

Maintenance

This stage in the lifecycle will now be a continual ongoing process. Errors will be found in every system, no matter how well it has been tested and these errors need to be addressed.

Ethically speaking, all software houses should maintain contact with their customers and offer a basic maintenance contract that also covers basic upgrades at no extra cost.

Increasingly more software houses offer expensive maintenance contracts to cover not only updates, but also on-site help and training.

Checkpoint 2

Explain why it is a good idea to run a new system in parallel with an older, outgoing system.

Checkpoint 3

Describe how the Internet has helped with the maintenance of software.

Exam questions   answers: page 130

The lifecycle of an ICT application includes these stages:

- Specification.
- Design.
- Implementation.
- Support and maintenance.

(i) (a) State at which stages the users of the application should be involved.

(b) Describe the nature of the user's involvement.

(ii) Some application developers believe that the specification must be agreed and fixed in detail before any other stage is considered. Others believe that modifications to the specification should be considered during the development process.

Discuss the relative merits of these two approaches.

(iii) Distinguish between testing and evaluation, and state at which stage they occur.   (40 min)

Organisational structure

Example

Requests for annual leave will be passed up the chain until they reach a level which includes the personnel function. They will then be passed down that chain and dealt with by administrative staff.

Any collection of people can be seen to form an organisation.

Organisations naturally form themselves into certain shapes, moulded by the culture and nature of their environment (in this case the nature of the business). Some structures are as follows:

Hierarchical

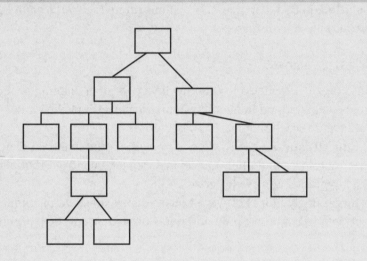

Features of hierarchical systems:

→ They are traditional.
→ They can be bureaucratic and slow to react/adapt.
→ There is usually a large chain of command.
→ They have a small span of control.
→ Roles and departments are clearly defined.
→ They allow for tight monitoring of 'subordinates'.
→ Generally discourage members from involvement across departments.

Horizontal

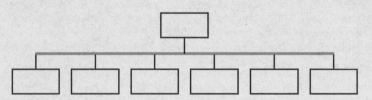

Features of horizontal systems:

→ They are more modern.
→ Information flows more quickly.

→ There is a smaller chain of command.
→ There is a larger span of control.
→ There is more reliance on the self-motivation of 'subordinates'.
→ They encourage members to become involved across departments.

Various paradigms ●●●

Geographical structure:

→ Used by multinationals.
→ Flat in the various countries of business.
→ Overall hierarchical.

Product structure or matrix:

→ Departments specialise in the design, marketing and sale of *one* product.
→ Compete against other product departments within the same organisation.
→ Discourages movement across teams.
→ Can be excessively competitive and stressful places in which to work.

Summary ●●●

Organisations and their structures can be indicative of the culture that they illustrate. Generally, hierarchical systems work on people 'knowing their place' and can react badly to unforeseen changes of any magnitude. On the other hand, horizontal systems tend generally to be more 'open' and react well to change as the members tend to be more multi-skilled and feel able to take on responsibility.

Example

Requests for annual leave. A form could be taken directly to personnel after being signed off by a line manager.

Checkpoint 2

Which of the two illustrated structures would lend themselves to operators being more involved in the decision-making process?

Checkpoint 3

How does being multi-skilled affect how an individual could perform within a structure?

Exam question   answer: page 130

WhyZ is a company that is structured hierarchically.

Describe the features of a hierarchical organisation.   (10 min)

Management Information Systems

The power offered by ICT systems can be ignored if action is not taken to use the data they make available. Management Information Systems were developed to tap this potential.

Definition ●●●

A system that manipulates data in order to produce meaningful information that will form the basis of decisions made by an organisation's management.

Management Information Systems rely heavily on query and report facilities.

Place in the organisation ●●●

There are three distinct levels of management:

→ Strategic.
→ Tactical.
→ Operational.

How MIS helps strategic management:

→ Statistics regarding population could help the process of decision-making when considering the opening of a new factory, etc.

How MIS helps tactical management:

→ Population and average income statistics could help a store manager decide on the new types and volumes of produce to stock in the grocery department of a supermarket, etc.

How MIS helps operational management:

→ Tracking the number of visits to the GP regarding sore throats could help the attached pharmacy decide to order more lozenges that particular week.

The quality of the information stored in the MIS will have an effect on the decisions made. Incorrect data can lead to expensive mistakes.

MIS has always been an important part of an organisation's work – now there are various ICT applications to aid the making of these decisions. Sometimes these are compiled into one application, similar to a large database, but on other occasions they are discrete applications that are used to carry out particular tasks, with the results being interpreted and presented in a specific package, such as a DTP application.

Checklist to maximise success ●●●

To make sure that a management information system functions to the advantage of the users a number of things must be considered:

Take note

Re-word this to make a definition you can recall easily.

Checkpoint 1

Which level of management does a manager who describes their role as policy development come from?

Examiner's secrets

Memorise these three levels – they are the building blocks of many MIS questions.

Links

See Value and importance of information, page 34.

Checkpoint 2

Which level of management would the member of school staff who works out the timetable be said to belong to?

- → Ensure an in-depth analysis has been undertaken.
- → Involve the end-users (i.e., management) in the design of the system – after all, they will be using it.
- → Treat the system as a whole – don't allow too much concentration on only the hardware/potential developments/low-level data processing, etc.
- → Development teams need to be kept on track – tight project management must be maintained to reach the budget and time targets set initially.
- → Train the end-users so they are aware of both the capabilities and limitations of an ICT system. This should lead to them not making unrealistic demands of the development team.
- → Ensure that professional standards are set and maintained.
- → Document everything – this will provide a clear source for reference – it will help the project team to establish changing end-user needs and will provide a source of technical reference for any future development.

Education is now supported by a complex and pervasive MIS. Many schools use a system called SIMS, which is basically a massive database. Within the database are records for each pupil and member of staff. The data is updated regularly with details of attendance, examination results, option choices and other information.

Unfortunately, many MISs are often designed to do a particular set of tasks, yet when put into service, the users soon start to require a greater set. As the MIS is an expensive system to set up, it is often added to, rather than scrapped and a new system put into place matching the new requirements. This can mean that the MIS is sometimes pushed beyond what it was designed to do, making it unstable and liable to 'lose' data. It is, therefore, essential that as much research of users' needs is carried out before the system is developed, and continual development is budgeted into the price of the system.

Checkpoint 3

Explain why it is important to document everything in a MIS.

Exam questions   answers: pages 130–1

1 The manager of a local company complains that the company's information continually fails to provide the correct level of information. State *four* possible reasons why the system is failing.   (6 min)

2 (a) What is meant by a management information system?
   (b) State *four* factors that could contribute to the success or failure of a management information system.   (15 min)

Decision support systems and executive

Data, once manipulated to form information, will usually be of some use to its end-user. Sometimes, further or more specialised manipulation of data is required and specialised systems exist to satisfy this need.

Types of decision

Structured or familiar

These are made on occasions where precedent has been set and the decision is made, based on previous knowledge of the expected outcome. This type of decision proves no problem for practised decision-makers.

Unstructured or unfamiliar

These are decisions that have to be made where there is no previous knowledge of an expected outcome. The amount of risk involved will play an important part in the decision-making process.

Decision support systems

These can take many forms but fundamentally they help a manager to make a decision by looking at the boundaries of a problem and predicting an outcome. The problem is simulated and manipulated so 100 per cent reliance on the decision offered would not be sensible. Many DSSs will have a range of contingency plans that can be seen as escape routes from bad decisions.

They are best employed in situations where the decision is unstructured but can be inferred. Expert systems may be used as DSSs.

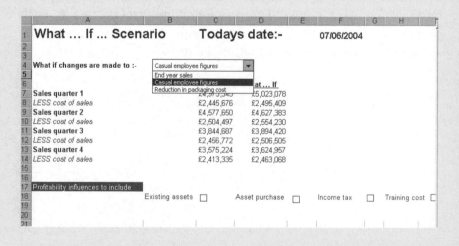

Executive information systems

These are a derivation of MIS. They summarise the MIS information further, to leave the viewers/users of the information (i.e., the strategic managers) with 'the bottom line'. The users are not concerned with how the data was produced, only with the figures produced by the EIS on which they will form their decisions.

Checkpoint 1

Why is there a need for decision support systems?

Links

See Expert systems and applications of artificial intelligence, page 112.

Checkpoint 2

Why would an executive be more interested in the EIS report, rather than the MIS report?

information systems

The end-users tend not to be very comfortable with computer systems so the design of EIS is very important. All of the data processing will be hidden and output needs to consist of exception reports and representative charts.

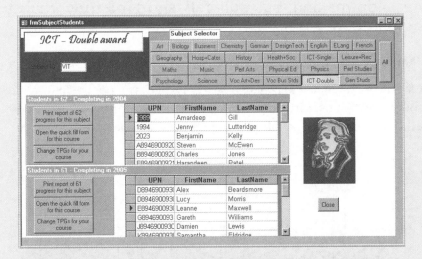

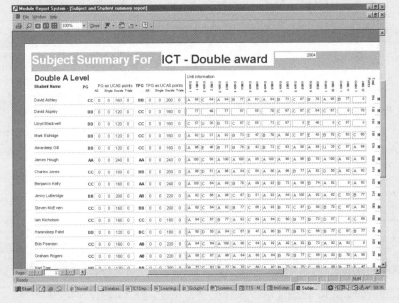

The images above show two views of a school MIS. The first is the database itself, showing the various fields, accessed via tabs, that show details of courses, students and staff, etc. The second image shows a report generated from the MIS data. This could be distributed to appropriate staff or other interested parties.

Exam questions   answers: page 131

The European Space Agency has to manipulate vast amounts of data to derive the results needed from scientific experiments. This data is sent through space as binary data.

(a) Describe the types of decisions made by the scientists when analysing the terabytes of data.   (10 min)

(b) Explain why the final results shown to the public could be considered to be an executive summary.   (10 min)

Expert systems
and applications of

Emulation by computer, of human activity is the stuff science fiction is made of. Expert systems and artificial intelligence applications are actual real-life instances of these emulations that are capable of advanced decision-making but still fall short of truly realistic human behaviour.

Checkpoint 1

Describe the difference between expert systems and artificial intelligence.

Expert systems – definition and diagram ●●●

An expert system (or knowledge-based system) is a pool of information, coupled with a user-friendly interface that allows for questions to be asked and replies to be inferred from the knowledge base.

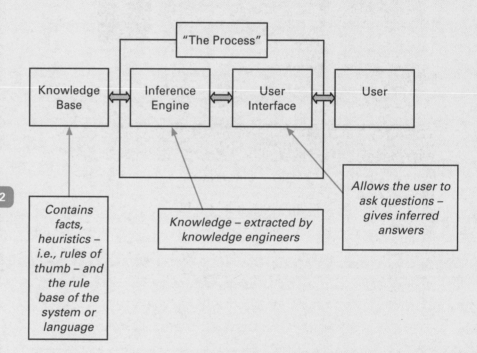

"The Process"

Knowledge Base ⟷ Inference Engine ⟷ User Interface ⟷ User

Contains facts, heuristics – i.e., rules of thumb – and the rule base of the system or language

Knowledge – extracted by knowledge engineers

Allows the user to ask questions – gives inferred answers

Checkpoint 2

How can the knowledge base affect the ability of a system to make decisions?

Examples of use ●●●

→ Medical applications for correct diagnosis and medication for complaints – MYCIN and ELSIE.
→ Configuration of computer systems – XconVAX.
→ Geological exploration – PROSPECTOR.

Many expert systems start life as 'shells' which can be adapted for any purpose that can be summarised into facts and heuristics. For example, the British Gas fault diagnosis system used for diagnosing boiler problems.

Examiner's secrets

Ethical questions may arise from this topic. Be prepared to talk about the effect of AI on employment, skills for work, etc.

artificial intelligence

Artificial intelligence – business applications ●●●

The design and use of hardware and software that acts in a way that may be deemed intelligent.

Highly used in industry to control robotics with set patterns and the limited intelligence of being able to stop processing independently.

→ Now used for a plethora of applications, e.g., speech synthesis and recognition, pattern learning, object recognition and visual interpretation.
→ The field is continually evolving as the programming environment becomes more flexible.
→ Until more is know about how humans learn and their brains develop, AI will be limited because it is these aspects of human behaviour AI tries to emulate.

Natural language development ●●●

The need to translate high-level programs into machine code restricts the syntax that can be used to program AI systems. The way that the computers respond to questioning will be based on the limitations of the language used to communicate – a limitation of its 'intelligence'.

Research is underway which will make it possible to 'talk' to a system using normal language. This will then be compiled and fed to the computer to process, possibly allowing us to see computers passing the Turing test.

Take note

Make a list of security applications that use AI, e.g., retina scanning etc.

Checkpoint 3

Why is it important to develop natural language processing?

Take note

Research the main elements of the Turing test.

Exam questions   answers: page 131

1 There is some evidence that certain specialist ICT systems are better at diagnosing illness than many highly respected medical consultants. Describe, with justification, *two* other applications of ICT that may be challenging the intellectual capabilities of the human species.   (8 min)
2 (a) What is meant by the term 'expert system'?
   (b) Describe *one* example of the use of an expert system.   (8 min)

Corporate information systems

Information technology and information systems were once a function of an organisation – the benefits reaped by their introduction raised their profile to the lofty heights of being part of corprate strategy and organisational direction.

Purpose of the corporate view

In order to grow and develop, an organisation needs to have strong leadership. As so much of the competitive advantage organisations find themselves with is directly related to their use and incorporation of ICT, it is only natural that ICT and IS should be corporate level issues.

Corporate strategy utilises what is called a PEST analysis to help make long-term decisions – this consists of a close examination of:

→ The *political* position.
→ The *economic* position.
→ The *social/environmental* position.
→ The *technological* position.

Each of these positions will be appraised using what is known as a SWOT analysis to establish:

→ Corporate **s**trengths.
→ Corporate **w**eaknesses.
→ Corporate **o**pportunities.
→ Corporate **t**hreats.

This shows that corporate-level decisions about technological change and development are as important as decisions relating to economics.

The reason for a corporate view is quite simple. If the rest of the organisation is busy with tactical and operational level management and decisions, competitive advantage may be lost. With the top level of management now making ICT and IS a corporate level issue, this is less likely to occur.

Many organisations, in the past, developed activities at the suggestion of certain departments, notably the marketing or sales departments. However, the advent of ICT systems that can manipulate large amounts of data has given greater control to the people in charge of the IS. As much of the data submitted to the IS probably comes from the marketing or sales department, things may not have changed as much as it may seem!

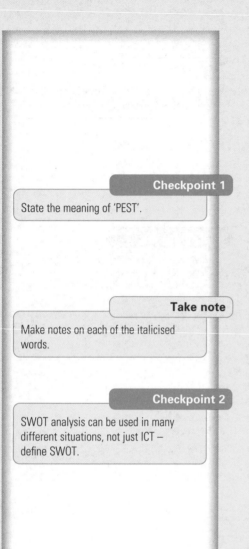

Checkpoint 1

State the meaning of 'PEST'.

Take note

Make notes on each of the italicised words.

Checkpoint 2

SWOT analysis can be used in many different situations, not just ICT – define SWOT.

Checkpoint 3

Long-term management systems are . . . ?

Influences of IS at a corporate level ●●●

IS can influence the direction of corporate-level decisions. However, this can only be the case if the information is presented in a suitable and appropriate manner, using formalised systems:

→ MIS.
→ EIS.

This will enable the decision-makers to understand the details and therefore make informed choices.

→ ICT provision based on more than the accountant's position of cost.
→ Applications of ICT are seen as more than simple data processing.

How information flows ●●●

Information flow is a crucial aspect of any organisation. It is important that everyone who needs information gets the correct information in the appropriate manner, at the correct time.

Data flow:

→ Depends on the organisational structure:
  → Hierarchical organisation – slow flow with slow reactions.
  → Horizontal organisation – quick flow with proactive reactions.
→ Depends on the systems in place:
  → Electronic, e.g., e-mail, bulletin boards, intranets, etc.
  → Verbal – via meetings, presentations, etc.
  → Documented – via newsletters, memos, etc.
→ Depends on the message:
  → Culture of the organisation – if the members are interested, information flows surprisingly quickly.
  → If dressed up too completely, it will not be understood and that may cause resentment.

Levels of management and their scope ●●●

The three types of management make decisions about different aspects of the organisation's future development:

→ Strategic – long-term, corporate decisions such as investing in e-commerce or not.
→ Tactical – medium-term decisions such as installing DVDs or not.
→ Operational – short-term decisions such as transmitting information via e-mail or bulletin boards.

Checkpoint 4

Medium-term management systems are . . . ?

Checkpoint 5

Short-term management systems are . . . ?

Take note

Make a list highlighting which types of ICT issues each of the levels of management would get involved with.

Exam question answer: page 131

Information systems are capable of producing strategic and operational level information. With the aid of examples, explain the difference between these two levels of information, clearly stating the level of personnel involved in using each one. (10 min)

Management of change

Take note

Change management involves understanding the level of change that a project will cause to its people, and proactively developing strategies and action plans to manage the impact of that change.

Check the net

Useful information on change management can be found on: www.westrek.hypermart.net/org

Checkpoint 1

Why must training be provided when change is to take place?

Action point

Change management is an important part of large corporations' training policies. Contact a large company to check this out. *Riding the Waves of Culture* (Economists books) explain how they work at this problem.

Checkpoint 2

Why is change management so important?

Take note

Change management can be expensive, so multinationals often prepare staff for change that other organisation, perhaps on low budgets, cannot.

In order to give the system the best chance of success, change needs to be managed effectively. This ranges from personnel functions regarding the individual's happiness in their job, through to the training department's approach to the teaching of new skills.

Skillbase and the effect on employment

→ Adequate training must be maintained.
→ More specialised workforce may evolve leading to a reduction in the number who are multi-skilled.
→ Decisions regarding ICT tend to be made by accountants who may ignore the human factor, e.g., savings by introducing a new system may not be equated to a reduction in workforce.
→ Older members of the workforce may feel unable to take on extensive training.

Organisational culture

→ Employees may feel so badly about a system that they resent change and ultimately damage the organisation.
→ Stratified skills could lead to a less individualised and creative workforce.
→ Exclusion from the development process will lead to a lack of understanding and may make the workforce feel inadequate – low self-esteem is not the basis for a healthy organisational culture.
→ Members with no vote or mandate may see areas they could contribute to, but become frustrated as their opinion doesn't count.
→ In 1989, due to the introduction of more effective systems alongside other corporate issues, BT 'lost' a whole tier of lower management. This was followed up in the early 1990s by the thinning of middle management in order to change a hierarchical system into a flatter organisation.
→ Members may become unsure of their roles and responsibilities.

Change management includes physical change (moving offices) to changes in technology.

For large companies change can be initiated by:

→ Technological advances.
→ Changes in policy.
→ Changes in work practice.
→ Political pressure.
→ Environment issues.
→ Staff restructuring.

Change management in ICT projects

Change management is a complex task, which normally requires substantial levels of resources and effort. It is a continuous process that must take place throughout all stages of a project and must have the commitment and support of the CEO and senior management.

This commitment and support must cascade down and the ultimate success of the implementation of the change will depend on:

→ High levels of effective sponsorship over the life of the project.
→ Effective marketing of the change which builds commitment within the company without unrealistically raising expectations.
→ Benefits that will be realised.
→ Recognising and managing resistance to the change through a continuous monitoring of the views and expectations of management and staff.
→ Management of change is concerned with the needs and aspirations of people and is a key element of project management.

Checkpoint 3

Which style of management – hierarchical or horizontal – would implement change in a more understanding manner?

Exam questions   answers: page 132

1   As a manager how would you help your staff cope with a major change to their basic software?   (10 min)
2   Successful change management focuses on managing the 'well being' of the people that are subject to the change. How would you achieve this goal?   (5 min)

Audits

In order to check that a system is working as it should, there may be occasion for the use of a tracking tool. Audits can help to clarify use or misuse and correct administration.

The legal position

→ A system that involves transactions must be audited by law. Auditors will look at the whole process and may track certain data through the system to ensure it is being processed correctly.

→ Financial record systems, e.g., invoices, orders, payroll etc., need to be audited once a year. This involves both computerised and paper records.

→ According to the Data Protection Act 1998, data must be kept secure – access may need to be audited if it comes to light that data is not held securely.

→ The Computer Misuse Act 1990 stipulates that unlawful entry is an offence. One of the best ways of gaining evidence will be via the use of audit trails that track every move made during logon.

How audits affect the data held

Generally, the use of audits has helped to improve the quality of data held.

It tends to be:

→ Accurate.
→ Complete.
→ Up-to-date.
→ Legal.
→ Non-libellous – the DPA and Freedom of Information Act mean that holders could face prosecution if holding untrue information about an individual. This has led to operators being more careful when making notes on correspondence with the individual.

Audit effects on data are not all positive: the use of encoding to act as a safeguard against accusation of inaccurate data has led to the individual being issued with lists of meaningless codes when they have requested to see copies of records held about them.

What they look for

When doing an ICT audit, companies need to look at areas such as networking and telecommunications, security management, application and system development, and systems architecture and models. They also need to take into account other factors, such as operations security, business continuity and disaster recovery plans, law investigations, and ethics and physical security.

Take note

The reason for not having this practice is partly because the organisations are not aware that a weakness in the system may exist or don't realise what is going on in the back-end.

Checkpoint 1

Would an online sales web site need to be audited?

"If the auditors don't understand the system, then they cannot discharge their duty well."

Malaysian Institute of Certified Public Accountants

Checkpoint 2

Is a misspelt address or name on a form against the law?

For an effective IS auditing, auditors need wide knowledge and understanding to interpret and present findings in a logical way, so that recommendations and rectifications can be done.

Audit trails

These are software procedures built in to make a note of login, access rights, action taken during login, etc., to track any fraudulent use or to protect the customer (recording of telephone conversations for training purposes) or to protect the user from accusation of fraud.

Rapid growth and constant change of computer information systems along with the take-up of business on the Internet requires that systems be continually re-evaluated in terms of their ability to maintain their integrity, thus making information security a fundamental business concern.

Disaster Recovery

For businesses one of the most important aspects of an audit of the ICT facilities will include a disaster recovery plan.

Disasters could be technical – virus infection, physical – fire, theft, or a combination – sabotage!

There are many companies offering disaster recovery as a service; they carry out an audit of organisations' ICT, then put together a plan for how to ensure that if something goes wrong, the organisation will be positioned to avoid too much inconvenience.

The disaster recovery plan will include;

→ A contingency audit – a survey of what is in place already – back-ups, secure log-ins.
→ A plan for putting measures in place, or improving the measures already in place – storing back-ups securely, off site.
→ A business impact survey, looking at what changes made to systems to avoid potential disasters will have on employees or clients – increased security can be off-putting.

The organisation can then choose to follow the suggested plan, making its systems more robust and secure, or adopt some of the measures, such as storage of back-ups, off site. Some risk may be acceptable, in some cases, but organisations such as financial institutions need to be completely safe from any attack, to ensure that the customers feel confident that their money is stored securely.

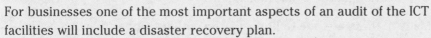

Example

Information security audits will help to identify those information assets that are most vulnerable, prioritise them in order of importance, and work out a security regime to ensure they are adequately protected.

Checkpoint 3

Describe an audit trail.

Exam questions   answers: page 132

1   Describe in detail, why an audit is an important aspect of ensuring that all is as it should be.   (10 min)
2   How are passwords and logins used in putting together an audit trail.

(10 min)

Disaster recovery

There is no way to truly guarantee that a system will not fail at some stage or other. The best that can be done is to use a system that is as secure as possible and couple this with a sound plan on how to recover after a disaster.

Threats

In setting up a disaster recovery plan, it important to first find out where the dangers, or threats, could come from:

➜ Negligence – lack of backup plan.
➜ Malicious damage – internal.
➜ Accidental damage, e.g., misplaced magnets.
➜ Natural disaster – fire, flood, earthquake.
➜ Illegal access – hacking, etc.
➜ Human error – transcription errors.
➜ Hardware failure – disk crash, etc.

Many of these are due to human intervention – rather than a machine 'destroying' data.

Risk analysis

The type of security and disaster recovery policy employed will depend on the importance placed on the following:

The nature of the data
➜ Strategic – there may be time to reconstitute this data without much disruption due to the long-term nature of the content and decision based on it.
➜ Tactical – may cause inconvenience and temporary financial loss.
➜ Operational – may cause the organisation to cease functioning altogether.

This reinforces the fact that corporate level ICT must be involved in aspects of the whole system, not just the parts that affect the corporate level of management.

Who has access to the system?
Groups of known individuals should pose less of a threat than users who utilise the system on a temporary basis. Therefore sufficient security and audit needs to be in place to deal with both types of user.

Financial losses arising from data loss

Once the impact of data loss has been quantified, decisions regarding the type of recovery procedures can be made. A simple yet stringent security system may be put in place or a service could be employed.

Most data recovery will cost money, therefore a simple calculation should be made: will recovering the data cost more than the value of the data?

Checkpoint 1

What is malicious damage?

Checkpoint 2

Whereas strategic management is seen as long term, the loss of strategic data may not be as serious as loss of operational data – why?

This type of calculation is often considered when companies decide on the type of insurance to be taken out and what facilities should be insured. Sometimes it could cost more to insure an item, than the item would cost to replace if it was damaged or stolen.

Disaster recovery services ●●●

There are a number of strategies available to a company or organisation. These are often available from third parties, for a fee.

→ **Reciprocal agreement** – an organisation of a similar size could be used to act as your server until your equipment is functioning again. This may be a free service offered by one organisation, under the agreement that if the same should happen to that organisation the first organisation will make the same offer.

→ **Cold standby** – a mirror image of your system held in a different location. These can be very expensive and are employed by users such as major utility companies. Many web sites are held on 'mirrored' servers, so that if something should happen to the main server site, users would be redirected to the mirrored version. This also gives the company the facility of updating their site, without causing any disruption to the users.

→ **Disk fixing service** – organisations that will extract your disks and attempt to salvage as much data as possible. This has interesting legal implications, as forensic investigations of computer systems have been carried out for a number of years now. Many criminal cases have come about because of data that has been recovered from hard disks. There are also positive benefits for organisations that fear the loss of important data, as the basic binary data that is stored on a disk can often be rebuilt, even after apparently catastrophic disasters.

Checkpoint 3

Which role or position in an organisation may be in charge of risk analysis?

Example

The crash of the Stock market networks in London on 5 April 2000 cost billions of pounds. It has been suggested the most likely cause of the failure was poor management.

Exam question   answer: page 132

Describe why it is important for all organisations, even small enterprises, to have considered disaster recovery. (10 min)

Legislative effects on information and

The day-to-day role and responsibilities attached to the ICT management of an organisation do not stop at ensuring that the system is operational. They will also be responsible for the enforcement of current legislation while keeping an eye on future developments.

Links

See Legal framework, pages 42–3.

Checkpoint 1

How many principles are there in the DPA?

Enforcing the Data Protection Act 1998

If records are to be kept concerning individuals who can be identified from the data, the holders are obliged to register with the Data Protection Registrar.

Non-compliance with the spirit of the eight principles of the Act, can lead to action being taken by the registrar and in more serious cases, civil actions being filed.

Certain sections of the Act are especially relevant to ICT management, for example the issues regarding security of data, its relevance, its correctness and how up to date it is.

Following a high-profile murder case, recently, the Data Protection Act is to be rewritten. This is to avoid evidence that could be used to protect the public being destroyed, following its use for other matters.

Enforcing the Computer Misuse Act 1990

Although the act offers protection against both the casual and intentional abuser, it is ultimately the organisation's responsibility to ensure that the levels of security employed are adequate for its needs.

Physical security

→ Offers protection for employees, e.g., security guards, security doors.
→ Protects property, e.g., locks for hardware.
→ Commonly combined to provide a sentry system of both security guards and hardware immobilising devices.

Checkpoint 2

Can the physical environment be covered by the Computer Misuse Act?

Logical security

→ Passwords – could be personal-user passwords or more complex, e.g., the systems used to check the identity of a telephone banker – parts of the personal identification number (PIN) used to operate cash machines may be asked for, or even other personal information that you gave the bank when opening the account, e.g., mother's maiden surname, memorable dates, etc.
→ Identification numbers or names given to the user by the system administrator.
→ Firewalls applied to systems using WANs or LANs with possible weak points, easily targeted by hackers.
→ Encryption of data so that, if hacked, it holds little interest and less value.
→ Retina scans, fingerprint and voice recognition – more hi-tech versions offering fine-tuned security.

Take note

One major oil producer will dismiss staff instantly if they put unauthorised software on their PCs. This has dramatically reduced the reported cases of commuter viruses.

communications technology

Contractual security

The majority of computer misuse occurs as a result of internal systems abuse. This has led to more and more organisations writing in a 'forced recognition' clause to employment contracts, outlining acceptable use and the consequences of unacceptable use.

If all of these security methods have been employed and computer misuse still occurs, the last step an organisation can take is to prosecute so that examples are made of misusers and legal precedent can be quantified.

Enforcing health and safety ●●●

All organisations need to ensure that health and safety directives are not only made into policy, but are followed by staff. To do this the following measures are suggested:

→ Organisation should have a designated health and safety representative.
→ Health and Safety Executive (HSE) is a government body with enforceable powers to extract compensation and custodial sentences for breaches of health and safety law.
→ Only purchase approved equipment that meets either the British (BS) or International (ISO) standard.
→ The representative should ensure that regular checks are carried out on the condition of equipment.

Employee obligations ●●●

An employee is bound by health and safety policies and guidelines. However, it is the employees' responsibility to ensure that they work in a safe manner:

→ Contractual obligations may mean that staff can only do certain things.
→ DPA requires confidential handling of data.
→ Health and safety laws require that the employee reports faults, does not create hazards or obstructions and that they use equipment for its intended purposes.

Check the net

Search for convictions under this act to get real examples that will embellish an exam answer.

Check the net

Look up their web site for descriptions of their roles and any previous actions regarding health and safety law.

Checkpoint 3

Who defines acceptable or unacceptable use for ICT equipment and resources in an organisation?

Exam question   answer: page 132

An organisation that has customer details stored on a computer system needs a security policy to protect that data.
Describe the main aspects that need to be covered by the policy, giving reasons why those aspects should be covered.   (20 min)

Project management

ICT systems tend to be complex collections of various subsystems incorporating hardware, software and the end-users. In order to produce systems that meet their original requirements, the role of project manager has evolved.

The role of project manager

The project manager needs to:

→ Take overall responsibility for the project's completion.
→ Schedule time and budget costs.
→ Analyse risk and identify opportunity.
→ Monitor project progress regarding schedules and budgets.
→ Manage, motivate and appraise the team.
→ Act as a point of contact for end-users, team members and clients.

This list of needs demands that a project manager be:

→ Technically competent with both analysis and programming skills.
→ A strong leader who can motivate and manage.
→ A trouble-shooter with excellent interpersonal skills.

Checkpoint 1

Does the project manager have to carry out all of the tasks mentioned?

Modules

Most projects these days are handled by small teams – this allows for the use of a modular approach. Each team member works on a small part or subsystem, enabling benefits such as:

→ The project manager can see the progress of each team member and identify strengths or weaknesses.
→ Allows for easier debugging as buggy modules can be identified, isolated and fixed simply.
→ Prototyping so the end-users/clients can monitor progress, etc.
→ Quick completion – modules placed together to produce the system.

Links

See System lifecycle models and Systems analysis and development, pages 102–5.

Checkpoint 2

How does a team structure help with a modular approach?

Documentation

This is a vital part of an effective project manager's remit – good quality documentation enables the manager to:

→ Produce a system blueprint that may be used for the creation of user manuals.
→ Target areas that require training among the end-users on all levels, e.g., technical through to occasional users.
→ Produce evidence that can be used as benchmarks when estimating future projects – timescales and budgets.
→ Analyse what has made a project a success or failure.

Tools

Gantt charts and critical path analysis (CPA) are two tools that have been used in traditional project management.

Gantt charts show the projected time required (with a space for the recording of actual time used) with areas of overlap, indicating when two or more jobs can be done at the same time and areas of 'slippage' where the project may be speeded up or slowed down with little effect on the deadline.

Checkpoint 3

Why is it important to evaluate the project upon completion?

Task	1	2	3	4	5	6	7	8
Meet with clients	▓							
	▓							
Choose hardware and install		▓	▓	▓				
		▓	▓					
Install software				▓	▓	▓		
			▓	▓				
Test software					▓	▓		
Train staff							▓	▓

CPAs show more detail and require you to break project tasks down and establish how long the task will take to complete. CPAs also require a comprehensive analysis of the order that certain tasks must take, e.g., training cannot precede hardware choice in a completely new system as the users require hardware to train on! The manager identifies the path that takes the longest amount of time to establish the 'critical path'.

Task	Description	Duration	Must follow
A	Analyse current system	2	
B	Produce DFDs	1.5	A
C	Meet client to discuss	0.5	B
D	Reuse DFDs	0.5	C
E	Select software	1	D
F	Install software	1.5	E
G	Train users	2	F

Exam questions   answers: pages 132–3

Large projects require very careful management. This can often be supported by ICT systems.

(a) Describe, giving examples, the data that a project management system would handle.   (10 min)

(b) Explain how a Gantt chart can help with managing a project.   (5 min)

Software development

Software development and engineering could be argued as being the most exciting and progressive areas in ICT. Software is required to bring all of the innovations in communications, networking, hardware, etc., to life.

CASE tools ●●●

Computer aided software engineering (CASE) tools is an area of current development. They are used to aid the processes of software engineering and cover such aspects as project management planning to the generation of code from libraries. The following table gives an idea of where CASE tools pop up.

Area of use	Examples of products
Project management	Scheduling, e.g., PERT and Gantt chart generators, CPA generators – MS Project
Analysis and design tools	Data-flow diagram generators
Programming tools	Application and report generators, fourth generation languages, e.g., Access, Lotus 1-2-3
Debugging and testing tools	Random data generators for test material
Documentation	CAD and RDBMS auto-documentation facilities
Prototyping	Modelling and simulation, e.g., Excel

Common methodologies ●●●

Different projects require different software development approaches. As a result of previous experience, some common methodologies have evolved and can be used either as structures in their own right, or as starting points for projects. Some examples of these are:

→ Systems lifecycle model covered previously in this chapter.
→ Prototyping – used when developing software in a 4GL environment as it can help end-users to visualise what both they and the developers have in mind when concrete systems requirements do not exist.
→ SSADM – structured systems analysis and design methodology. An established method of systems development that generally finds use in large projects – favoured by government departments as a design methodology.
→ SSM – soft systems methodology. A methodology developed by Peter Checkland to deal with systems that do not have an obvious or clearly defined solution.

Checkpoint 1

Define the term 'CASE'.

Checkpoint 2

Why would a prototype of a system be developed?

Checkpoint 3

Define the term 'bug'.

Testing

Testing exists both as a software development tool – to see if a product works – and as a benchmark for purchasers. When you buy a piece of software, you presume that no serious bugs will exist because a series of tests will have been carried out. These tests are:

White box testing

Test the program structures and attempt to test each possible path that may be encountered to see if the program stands up to use.

Black box testing

Testing designed to try out the inputs, processes and outputs to see how well they operate using normal, invalid and extreme test data.

Alpha testing

Testing undertaken in-house to see that the whole piece of software works, i.e., white and black box tests combined.

Beta testing

The use of trusted third parties to test and evaluate software prior to general release.

Evaluation

The management team of an ICT department need to evaluate software or systems to ensure that all possible options have been considered before a choice is made for purchase. They will probably evaluate against some or all of the following criteria:

→ Is it upgradable?
→ Is it compatible with existing systems (both hard- and software)?
→ Are current system resources adequate?
→ Is it straightforward to use and learn?
→ What type of support is offered? Technical and manual based?
→ Cost and its affordability?
→ Does it operate at an adequate speed?
→ If any benchmarks have been applied and their results?

The results of these evaluations will be recorded and reported in an evaluation report.

Checkpoint 4

When would the public be involved in testing software?

The jargon

Benchmarks – tests run by bodies that have an interest in the product's performance, e.g., computer magazines may benchmark test the performance of several different VDUs against predetermined measures.

Exam question   answer: page 133

Many computer games use similar software elements or 'game engines'. Discuss the advantages and disadvantages of using an existing game engine when developing a new game.   (20 min)

Policy and strategy issues

When ICT was first introduced on a wide scale, it was seen as a tool to help in the administration of jobs and did not command much respect from senior management. Over time, it has raised its profile to the position we find it in now where it is seen as one of *the* major corporate policy issues.

The jargon

USP – unique selling point.

Checkpoint 1

Is a home user of ICT likely to be under 'end-user' or 'Centralised' control?

Take note

According to the experts most systems fail due to poor requirement gathering.

Checkpoint 2

Why is it important for a company's product to stand out from the crowd?

Use of ICT to gain competitive advantage ●●●

Every product and organisation needs to have a clearly identified USP that makes them and their product stand out from the crowd. As manufacturing has grown, it is more and more difficult for organisations to obtain and maintain their competitive advantage so many have turned towards the use of ICT to give them this unique advantage.

→ ICT can be used to offer a novel customer service experience.
→ ICT can be used to cut human resource costs.
→ Money saved may be ploughed back into research and development for new, technologically superior products.
→ ICT can also be used in the field of knowledge management where data and information are used in a manner that allows customer profiles and specific targets to be created for marketing purposes.

End-user computing ●●●

This is a specific discipline of ICT that tries to suggest the best way of introducing it in organisations. It is best illustrated by a synopsis of the two extremes:

Centralised ICT control

All choices regarding ICT are made by a designated 'ICT department'. In extreme cases, the end-users of the systems are not considered or consulted, but find the systems foisted upon them and adapt themselves to the systems' capabilities and limitations.

End-user computing

System choices are made by the end-users. This can range from choosing hardware through to developing their own systems – maybe via generic software. Although this does encourage autonomous working practices, in extremes it can lead to huge data redundancy and pockets of employees that find it difficult to integrate with their colleagues and eventual loss of control and direction.

ICT for strategic planning ●●●

This occurs on two main levels: software and business.

Software

Data can be manipulated through MIS and with the help of expert systems and decision-support systems can provide useful information to aid strategic plans and decisions.

Business

Recently set up organisations (mainly in the service industry) rely very heavily on ICT. They have no customer-facing offices and all business takes place either via telecommunications and call centres or over the Internet using e-commerce.

Emulation or wholesale replacement? ●●●

In corporate strategy, the issue of cost raises its head on many occasions. This, coupled with the length of time that an organisation views as 'the long term', will be considered when making a choice between costly capital investment that involves the replacement of equipment and software or the implementation of software that allows for emulation of existing systems, so they appear and act in the desired manner.

There are pros and cons associated with both methods:

→ *Replacement* – although costly allows for organisation-wide standardisation.
→ *Emulation* – relatively inexpensive and encourages developers to be cross-platform orientated when creating new systems, but it is not 100 per cent convincing or efficient.

Policy Management ●●●

Organisations must ensure that each aspect of its systems are covered by policies that are adhered to by all those involved.

When compliance and risk management are crucial, there are software systems that can be employed to ensure staff have read, understood and signed-up to key policies.

Issuing policy via intranet or email could mean that although it is made available, staff do not actually read it, or take notice of it. However these software management systems can help to solve this, by monitoring how the policy files are handled. They can be set to record automatically employees' understanding and acceptance, by having feedback forms, or simple user agreement buttons; this ensures that policy documents are not ignored. It can also ensure that the right policies get to the right people. They also create a permanent policy management audit trail.

Checkpoint 3

Decisions to make change can be instigated from which two areas?

Checkpoint 4

Define the term 'emulation'.

Exam question   answer: page 133

In developing an ICT strategy, an organisation must consider many things. List *three* factors that influence the development of an ICT strategy, and for each of these state some of the factors that the organisation should take into consideration.   (20 min)

Answers
Information and communications technology management

Systems lifecycle models

Checkpoints

1 There is no definite end, the process can be restarted and continually refined.
2 If deadlines are missed the whole process can be put into jeopardy, scope creep can occur, causing cost and time implications.
3 Spiral, as prototypes are developed and refined by the same team.

Exam question

Development of a system:
- Detailed brief set, specification drawn up and aspects devolved to appropriate teams.
- Market research team set brief to design data collections system and collect data.
- Software developers tasked with writing bespoke database to hold research responses.
- Data entry team enter data to check system.
- Security team employed to set up secure passwords and firewalls, backups and data storage.
- System tests carried out.
- Working system passed to customer with maintenance schedule.

Systems analysis and development

Checkpoints

1 Whole-system investigation, covering a great deal of research, high expertise of analysts but no end-product, that good analysis comes from the development of a better system.
2 New system can be monitored and bypassed if it begins to fail, improvements can be monitored, staff can be familiarised with new system, while working on familiar system.
3 Live updates, online message boards, downloading of patches to repair damaged or inefficient software.

Exam questions

(i) (a) Users should have input at the specification, support and maintenance stages.

At specification:
- Full involvement with the proposal for layouts on user interfaces (input and output).
- Agreement of the functionality of the project.
- Agreement of projected costs, estimated time scales and other contractual matters.

At support and maintenance:
- Help from and advice desk.
- Structured feedback on performance.
- In receipt of details of reported problems.
- In receipt of bus fixes and upgrades.

(ii) *Merits of approach 1*:
- Development teams are all clear about the next stage of work.
- The end-users can have updates stating the actual project purposes.
- Deadlines more likely to be met as 'last minute' developments would not be considered.

Merits of approach 2:
- Tends to encourage more creative software development.
- Prototyping is permissible, allowing the end-user access to the system prior to project completion.
- Constant review means changes to the development team are not too damaging.

(iii) Testing is part of the system implementation and is involved with the assessment of predetermined and planned data within the system to see if any bugs can be found. The reaction of the system to these tests needs to be documented and forms the basis of improvements to the system. Testing includes both black and white box tests and does not include the opinions of end-users. Evaluation is the summarisation of a system by comparing actual outcomes with the outcomes and objectives set at the start of the project. The end-user is involved heavily as their acceptance of the system is usually a good indication of success or failure.

Organisational structure

Checkpoints

1 Hierarchical.
2 Horizontal.
3 Ability to take on different responsibilities, offer advice to others, take part in informed discussions.

Exam question

Features of a hierarchical organisation are:
- It is arranged in a pyramid with the more powerful/ influential people at the top.
  The three major layers are:
- represented by management workers at the top;
- information workers below them;
- production workers at the bottom/lowest level.

Management information systems

Checkpoints

1 Strategic.
2 Operational.
3 Reference materials, to be used as the project develops, to help inform future developments.

Exam question 1

System failure could be caused by:
- Inadequate analysis.
- Lack of management involvement at design stage.
- Lack of end-user involvement.
- Too much emphasis on low-level data processing.
- Lack of management knowledge of ICT systems and their capabilities.
- Inappropriate management demands.
- A lack of professional standards.
- Needs adaptive maintenance.
- Insufficient training.
- Resistance to change.

Exam question 2

(a) A management information system converts data from both internal and external sources into information. It involves the communication of information to managers at different levels, in an appropriate form throughout an organisation.
It also enables effective decisions to be made, plans to be laid down and monitoring/control of performance.

(b) See the answer given for Question 1.

Decision support systems and executive information systems

Checkpoints

1 Management need to make decisions, some of which may be unstructured and have a level of risk, to minimise the risk, a system is needed to help make the decision.
2 MIS report contains too much information for most executives, they need the facts only.

Exam questions

(a) Structured or familiar decisions for data that is known – control data. Unstructured or unfamiliar decisions for analysing data from sensors.

(b) The detail received from the sensors gives far more detail than the general public will need, therefore the scientists put together a summary, containing images and 'headlines'.

Expert systems and applications of artificial intelligence

Checkpoints

1 Expert systems require the intervention of a human to move on decision-making, AI can make their own, independent decisions.
2 With greater knowledge a system can consider more options, and therefore make better grounded decisions.
3 A computer-based language will not convey the intricacies of human language, so machines will not be able to respond as humans do to a stimulus.

Exam question 1

Applications such as chess programs and financial advice systems, where the user is challenged by the system's reacting in a manner that makes it difficult for the user to be 100 per cent sure that the system is making 'decisions'. The applications that do this best, work in a non-predictive or pattern-based application.

Exam question 2

(a) The term 'expert system' means knowledge built into the system as a set of rules (i.e., knowledge base). Rules are held as data, updated by use (i.e., inference engine).
'contains the knowledge and replicates the performance of a human expert'.

(b) Prospector
The use of a knowledge base of geological data that can be queried to give a probability of certain ores or oil deposits being situated close to certain geological characteristics.
XCON VAX
An expert system that suggests configurations of computer systems based on predictions made from previous experience of successful configurations.

Examiner's secrets

Any other expert or knowledge-based system you have researched will do as long as you mention the concept of prediction or previous knowledge.

Corporate information systems

Checkpoints

1 Political, economic, social, technological.
2 Strengths, weaknesses, opportunities, threats.
3 Strategic.
4 Tactical.
5 Operational.

Exam question

Strategic decisions are often made with little consideration of implications – they are, therefore, usually made by very senior management. Once the strategic decision has been arrived at, the operational staff then take over, and these are usually managed by a senior member of the management. They will try to develop a method of achieving the strategy. Both of these layers of decision-making must be supported with accurate and appropriate information. A college principal deciding upon a strategic move to a new centre, will need information regarding the needs of the public in that area. The operational manager will then need to have access to information on budget, staffing requirements, possible funding opportunities and so on.

Management of change

Checkpoints

1 Staff need new skills to adapt to the change. Knowledge makes the change easier.
2 Ensures that everyone involved feels comfortable with the proposed change and therefore helps improve morale, thereby improving quality of outcome.
3 Horizontal.

Exam question 1

The installation and use of a new software application would start with attempting to get the staff involved with identifying the application specification. This would give them a level of ownership, prior to the change taking place, it would also give them time to come to terms with the change. Once the software had been installed, it is essential that all staff who would be using the software, be trained in its operation. There should also be a period of time after installation, where the software support was instant, either in person, or by telephone. In time this could be scaled down to online or e-mail support.

Exam question 2

All change is stressful, it is essential for change to be successful so that those affected by it feel that it is a positive thing. Staff should be shown how much better their job will be after the change, or how their work/life balance will be improved. Unfortunately this cannot always be possible, but positive, well-motivated staff generally achieve a higher quality of output, so it is worth trying.

Audits

Checkpoints

1 Yes – it has transactions.
2 No – it is how it is dealt with or used that may break laws.
3 Following a piece of data through a typical transaction, from initial request to delivery of outcome.

Exam question 1

Audits take a snapshot of a system – they can look at one aspect in detail, or all aspects. Each stage in a design and implementation cycle should be audited so that if something later goes wrong, it can be checked back to find where the error may have first appeared.

Exam question 2

An audit trail will take account of all points that a particular user has accessed a machine or application; this can then be used to check that this occurred at the appropriate times.

Disaster recovery

Checkpoints

1 Damage caused on purpose, vandalism, theft.
2 Strategy is long term, so data can be redeveloped, operational is immediate, so there is no time for recovery.
3 The network manager.

Exam question

All organisations have important data that should be protected; this may not be just electronic data. Each year every organisation must make a detailed return to the tax office. It is essential that the information used is accurate and kept safely for a number of years. If provision is not made for this, the tax office may dispute the figures and the organisation would not be able to prove the accuracy. There are also records such as customer or supplier details that, if lost, could be very difficult to replace. Each of these instances must be considered, and an effective strategy put in place to ensure that the data was safely stored.

Legislative effects on information and communications technology

Checkpoints

1 Eight.
2 Yes – security doors, locks on hard disks.
3 The management – each organisation needs to define their own benchmarks.

Exam question

Data stored on a computer system is covered by the DPA, therefore all organisations are legally responsible to fulfil the obligations that the DPA requires. This will ensure that any data stored will not, intentionally, be misused. Organisations also need to have physical security systems, such as locked doors, secure entry systems, security guards and lockable storage systems. These are set up to protect the data and the staff. There are also electronic systems (logical systems) such as logins and passwords, encrypted data and firewalls as well as other devices such as retinal scans, etc., that are used to prevent unapproved users accessing the data. Most organisations also have some sort of contractual limits on what employees are allowed to do, such as which aspects of a system they have access to. Each of these systems are put in place to control which employee has access to particular data.

Project management

Checkpoints

1 No, many of these can be delegated.
2 Team members can be set particular closed tasks, that then get fed back to the other members.
3 To ensure lessons are learned for future projects.

Exam questions

(a) The project management software would usually handle:

- Dates – deadlines, start points, crucial points.
- Times – finer details for deadlines, meeting times.
- Contacts – staff and others taking part in the project.
- Resources – staff and equipment, or facilities.
- Costs – financial records on budget, expenditure and profit.
- Gantt chart – diagrammatic display of the project.

(b) A Gantt chart is a visual representation of a project. It shows in graphical form the important aspects of the project. It allows the project manager to view the activities that are scheduled to take place at a particular point. The chart is made up from bars representing activities. These can be moved, overlapped or altered to produce the most efficient pathway through the project.

Software development

Checkpoints

1 Computer aided software engineering – using computers to generate code that can be used within a software environment to carry out a specific task.
2 To test aspects of the system, before installing it for real.
3 A mistake or error in a software system, that causes the system to produce further errors.
4 Possible at Beta testing stage, otherwise they would not be used.

Exam question

Using an existing game engine when developing a new game has advantages and disadvantages:
Advantages: Costs are kept lower as much of the development has been done on earlier engine design. Enables developers to present sequels to successful games without developing new games from scratch.

The engine can be licensed to other developers, bringing income from royalties.
Disadvantages: Produces games that are similar in play experience.
Can limit spontaneity in game design as the developers have to stick to the variables within the engine design. Development of first generation games is expensive as the game engine must also be developed.

Policy and strategy issues

Checkpoints

1 End-user.
2 To attract customers, and generate income.
3 Software and business.
4 Copying one system onto another so that the operator can work with the same data, in the same way on different systems.

Exam question

The organisation must consider:
Competitive advantage

- Are the competitors already using ICT? If so is it successful?
- Will the use of ICT speed up operations?
- Will the use of ICT offer customers something that other competitors do not presently offer?

Human resources

- Will staff need retraining? Are there likely to be fewer staff needed to carry out tasks?
- Are staff costs going to increase or decrease?
- Will the changes have an effect on morale?

Software and hardware procurement

- Is the hardware available/reliable? Is software available to carry out the operations needed?
- How much will it cost to purchase and maintain the equipment?
- Will it be cost effective to purchase or lease the equipment?

Revision checklist
Information and communications technology management

By the end of this chapter you should be able to:

1	Understand that every system requires conception, design, building, establishing, maintenance and evaluation.	Confident	Not confident **Revise** page 102
2	List the advantages and disadvantages of the use of a spiral, water and cycle system.	Confident	Not confident **Revise** pages 102 and 103
3	Discuss what is meant by a feasibility study and understand why one would be carried out.	Confident	Not confident **Revise** page 104
4	Understand why organisations form themselves into certain shapes.	Confident	Not confident **Revise** pages 106 and 107
5	Understand why the customer becomes involved again in the project at the implementation stage.	Confident	Not confident **Revise** page 109
6	Describe the reasons why a system should be evaluated.	Confident	Not confident **Revise** page 105
7	Understand place in organisations. There are three distinct levels of management.	Confident	Not confident **Revise** page 108
8	Describe the types of decision: structured or familiar.	Confident	Not confident **Revise** page 110
9	Write down the checklist to maximise success.	Confident	Not confident **Revise** page 112
10	Understand how organisations manage change and why this happens.	Confident	Not confident **Revise** pages 116 and 117
11	Understand why companies have audits and the legal issues involved.	Confident	Not confident **Revise** page 118
12	Be clear about what an audit trail is and how one is carried out.	Confident	Not confident **Revise** page 119
13	Describe disaster recovery including the threats and risk analysis.	Confident	Not confident **Revise** pages 120 and 121
14	Understand why different projects require different software development approaches and list these clearly.	Confident	Not confident **Revise** page 126
15	Explain the testing processes during software development.	Confident	Not confident **Revise** page 127

Interaction

The way in which humans interact with computers and information technology is fundamental to the design of the machines, their environs and the information or applications they offer.

Without considering interaction, failure would be inevitable, people could not work with the machines efficiently, the environments in which the machines are used might be unsuitable and the software might be unworkable. Training is all-important as new workers start to use ICT and as technology relentlessly moves forward. Simply understanding how ICT works is not enough. Humans need to use ICT efficiently and this would be a priority in the training programmes of many large companies. This new technology has brought with it new problems, workers abusing systems, crime and irresponsible usage. Therefore new codes of conduct have had to be drawn up.

Exam themes

→ Human–computer interaction and interface

→ Design of the human–computer interface

→ User support and training

→ Effective presentation of information and data

→ Information and the professional

→ Codes of conduct

→ Matching user requirements to the solution

→ Critical appraisal of information and communications systems

Topic checklist

○ AS ● A2

	OCR	EDEXCEL	AQA
Human–computer interaction and interface	●	○	○●
Design of the human–computer interface	●	●	●
User support and training	●	●	●
Effective presentation of information and data	●	●	●
Information and the professional	●	●	●
Matching user requirements to the solution	●	●	●
Critical appraisal of information and communications systems	●	●	●

Human–computer interaction and interface

The way in which a user interacts with a system is very important. If the system is to be accepted and successful, it is vital that users are confident in the environment. Developments in interface design have made systems easier to interact with and users more confident.

Requirements interpretation

The BCS computer magazine (January 2000) stated that a recent study found the single most influential factor in the success or failure of a system to be the interpretation of the end-user's requirements.

The physical

→ Eyestrain – caused by incorrect positioning of desks, VDUs, lights, etc., or by bad VDU design (need to be adjustable with contrast and brightness controls).
→ Stress – caused by having to work with uncomfortable/ non-ergonomic furniture and hardware.
→ Environmental factors – radiation from screens, carcinogenic exposure from toner in printers, photocopiers, etc.

The psychological

Factors that influence how well a system can be worked with (see Familiarity below).

Familiarity

Software developers are making more and more programs where common interfaces are seen, e.g., suites of programs all have similar icons and reactions to errors, etc. This is now being extended to other products that are produced by the same software house. They:

→ Satisfy the psychological factors governing the success or failure of a particular interface by the way the user interacts.
→ Make users more confident – a qualitative measure of success.
→ Use visual, aural, tactile and special (proximity and movement) aids to build familiarity, e.g.:
   → Visual – icons.
   → Aural – sounds in response to actions.
   → Tactile – mouse and keyboard clicks to activate items.
   → Special – movement of cursor, buttons depressing when clicked.

Icons

Their use is becoming increasingly common.

→ Must be meaningful.
→ Give help to novices.
→ Act as shortcuts for more expert users.
→ Slow down response times of the system as they use more resource than command lines.

The jargon

RSI – repetitive strain injury is an injury suffered by keyboard users; correct posture and well-designed wrists rests can help. If and when voice recognition software is perfected this type of injury could be reduced.

Checkpoint 1

What did the BCS state as the single most influential factor in the success or failure of a system?

Checkpoint 2

How does cost affect the number of non computer-literate users starting to use computers?

Take note

There is currently no agreed-upon definition of the range of topics which form the area of human–computer interaction.

Checkpoint 3

Why is icon design important in helping novices?

The jargon

Ergonomics – the study of physical factors in the work environment on performance.

Libraries of pre-set designs ●●●

→ O/S utility that offers interface attributes that have been chosen as they co-ordinate well, e.g., colour combinations for windows, fonts that suit the user.
→ Fun desktops with themes that cover both text styles and windows attributes and icon/sound features.
→ The libraries can be added to, with user-defined defaults. This gives the user ownership of the working area on screen as well as surrounding it.

Items for consideration in good design ●●●

→ Response speed – one-tenth of a second to complement the time it takes a human to recall from long-term memory.
→ Online assistance to help all levels of user.
→ Easy to remember commands.
→ Easy to use, i.e., intuitive.

The effects of developments ●●●

Human–computer interaction is, in the first instance, affected by the forces shaping the nature of future computing. These forces include:

→ Decreasing hardware costs leading to larger memories and faster systems.
→ Miniaturisation of hardware leading to portability.
→ Reduction in power requirements leading to portability.
→ New display technologies leading to the packaging of computational devices in new forms.
→ Assimilation of computation into the environment (e.g., VCRs, microwave ovens, televisions).
→ Specialised hardware leading to new functions (e.g., rapid text search).
→ Increased development of network communication and distributed computing.
→ Increasingly widespread use of computers, especially by people who are outside of the computing profession.
→ Increasing innovation in input techniques (e.g., voice, gesture, pen) combined with lowering cost, leading to rapid computerisation by people previously left out of the 'computer revolution'.
→ Wider social concerns leading to improved access to computers by currently disadvantaged groups (e.g., young children, the physically/visually disabled, etc.).

> **Take note**
>
> Human–computer interaction is a discipline concerned with the design, evaluation and implementation of interactive computing systems for human use and with the study of major phenomena surrounding them.

Exam question   answer: page 150

Employers should provide workers with a safe and comfortable working environment thus ensuring high productivity and less sickness.
When planning workstations what measures should they put in place?

(16 min)

Design of the human–computer interface

In order to get the most out of using a computer, it is important to be able to use it with confidence and competence. Developments in interface design have allowed many users to work in a competent manner with little or no real knowledge of how the machine works.

History ●●●

Computers were originally operated by utilising a series of punched cards. Once the system had started there was little or no chance of interaction. In the late 1960s, the operating system was introduced to aid control of running jobs and to speed up processing.

There were no seminal developments in end-user interaction until the introduction of disk operating systems (DOS) in 1967 where the user could take control of the computer's actions by typing commands in at a prompt. Although this was a great breakthrough, the system was still dependent on very competent users to operate it efficiently.

In 1981 the BBC commissioned a personal computer, to support their first attempts at producing television programmes, intended to educate the public. It had 16 k of memory – 16,000 spaces to store data; modern machines often have 1GB of memory – 8,000,000,000 spaces, and that is usually supported by millions of other data points.

The people capable of using the BBC for anything other than simple operations soon knew more than the TV presenters!

Many early computer users had to program the machine to do certain operations, or buy recorded programs that were loaded via cassette tape. Experts made many predictions, such as the end of the printed book by 1990! But because of the skills and knowledge needed to get the machine to do anything, most people could not see computers being as popular as they are today.

Menu Development ●●●

Data processing's popularity in the commercial sector led to the use of computers on a widespread basis. These users were in not hobbyist or expert users of computers, so more and more systems were developed that were navigated via use of menu structures that required the user to enter certain shortcut commands.

Eventually menus were developed where the cursor keys could be used to choose an option and activate it.

Menu systems were helpful to an extent but still required the user to know the path of menu choices that had to be made in order to get to the destination.

Graphical User Interface ●●●

As a result of studies into human/computer interaction, headway was made into designing systems that acted in a much more intuitive manner and graphic or graphical user interfaces were developed by Apple Macintosh in the 1980s.

These are complemented by a WIMP environment:

→ WIMP – windows, icons, menus and pointers.
→ WIMP – windows, icons, mouse and pop-up/pull-down menus.

Today these can be found on every type of personal computer.

GUIs offer the user ownership of their workplace. They offer a comfortable environment in which users feel in control and afford users a level of expertise without needing to know much about the system itself.

Modern GUI designs often allow the user to adjust properties such as backgrounds, icons and layout. However, many networked computers have this facility removed, as maintenance of systems that are identical is quicker and more straightforward than trying to reorganise a range of different settings.

Pictures

→ **Command line** – the arrow head cursor that appears when you try to start a PC with a floppy disc in the disc drive! Showing how computers were before Windows, e.g., BBC Micro:

```
BBC Computer 32
KBasic
>_
```

→ **Menu** – A list of items that offer a choice to a user:

→ **GUI** – Windows desktop – or Apple:

Checkpoint 2

Define the term GUI.

Checkpoint 3

What is the major difference for the user between DOS systems and Windows-based systems?

Exam questions   answers: page 150

1   Why has the development of a GUI enabled the general public to take advantage of computer technology?   (15 min)
2   Describe common menu structures accessible to users of a word-processing application.   (10 min)

User support and training

Systems that are put in place can only operate as effectively as the work force that use them. Through high-quality support and training, the management of an organisation can ensure that employees are in a position to get as much out of their system as they put into their employees.

Developer support

Operators and data processors are not the only users that need support – we will be looking at some strategies to support them later. Attention needs to be passed to the higher power end of the user market – the software and applications developers. Some of the tools available include:

→ Self-documenters.
→ CASE tools.
→ Compiler debuggers.
→ Catalogued run-time error libraries with advice.
→ Patches/releases.

In addition to this, developers are encouraged to seek certification for all of their professional development, e.g., MCSD Microsoft Certified Software Developer.

Documentation

Many forms of user documentation exist, including:

→ Manuals and user booklets.
→ Online context sensitive help (office assistant).
→ Worked examples or tutorials as a learning tool.
→ Magazines available in the High Street.
→ Bulletin boards and user forums on the Internet.

Types of training

Various types exist and can be used alone or in any combination depending on the trainee's needs.

→ Computer-based training – CBT, CAL or CAI. This is undertaken individually and is relatively inexpensive. It can be convenient as learning can be done in your free time and may be stopped and restarted many times.
→ Video and interactive video training. This form can have some degree of success but tends to be limited as the trainee has no true feedback and the learning tends to be task, rather than skills, based.
→ Online tutorials. Again, this can be task based and rarely results in the user being able to give an exact fit solution to a problem – it also tends to be an advertising tool for the new or best aspects of the software!

→ Step through books. The trainee works alone with very task-based scenarios, but books can prove an excellent future resource.

→ Instructor-led/classroom-based courses. Discussion and feedback occurs which enable the trainees to question their progress and learning. Tasks may be used as a starting point but skills soon develop. Unfortunately, these courses are time consuming and expensive.

Training as a strategic consideration ●●●

Job satisfaction is qualitative and as such, corporate management teams find it difficult to judge in their employees. They can also be surprised by the level of loyalty they can expect from their workforce. All this makes training a very expensive option and in more than one way.

What if employees use the organisation to pay for training and then set up freelance? Is it worth investing vast amounts of cash in someone who would leave when adequately 'tooled up'?

But, conversely, what if employees are not trained? Will this lead to low morale and self-esteem eventually manifesting as low levels of motivation?

On a more pecuniary level, we must remember that when employees are being trained they are costing money, not making it.

It would appear that adequate and relevant training of all employees on all levels is the best option with certification to prove they have the skills they claim, e.g. MOUS – Microsoft Office User Specialist; ECDL – European Computer Driving Licence endorsed by the BCS.

<aside>
Checkpoint 3

When an employee is being trained they are costing money not making it – what is meant by this statement?
</aside>

<aside>
Exam questions   answers: page 150

1   Why is it in the interest of employers that they should have a well-trained workforce?   (10 min)
2   How could an employer train staff to work with software? What methods are viable?   (18 min)
</aside>

Effective presentation of information and data

Information can be presented in many ways. The methods used often influence the viewer's perceptions of the information itself. Information presented in a haphazard manner or unprofessional in its appearance will reduce its impact. Informal presentation has its place and indeed may be necessary, for example in brainstorming and other creative activities sessions.

The dominant idea or concept or relevant piece of information should jump out at the audience immediately. This rule applies to designing a form, database or piece of typography. Data that is difficult to take in or understand equals poor quality information.

Information displays

Complex or 'busy' information displays will put people off. We are all lazy viewers when it comes to reading messages and if it is difficult to read we often do not bother. Text or graphics need space in order to be understood. Spreading elements out and making everything as large as possible for quick, easy viewing is a good rule of thumb. Good examples are posters on escalators – you usually have about two or three seconds to take in the entire message, therefore a mass of text or numbers will not work. Designers use space to draw your eye to focus on the message.

Typography

Use only one font and use upper- and lower-case letters. Sans serif faces such as Arial when projected for PowerPoint presentations are easier to read than serifed faces such as Times New Roman. Serifs are the tiny flicks on the top and bottom of a typeface such as Times – the idea is that the serifs help the eye follow the line of text. Most newspapers and paperbacks are printed using a serifed typeface.

We use colours to contrast, highlight and differentiate categories, separate groups of data or call attention to a key point. In general for PowerPoint-type presentations, light-coloured text against a dark background is easier to read from a distance than dark text on a light background. However, on paper, black in white offers the most readability.

When DTP first arrived many people got carried away with the abilities of the software to generate so many typefaces that they used the lot. The consequence was that many in-house notes or newsletters became difficult to read. Mixing too many typefaces, such as italic and bold and various fonts, creates excessive contrast and slows reading.

Take note

Lower-case fonts are easier to follow than upper-case fonts as they look more like handwriting. Upper-case fonts have more to do with ancient chiselled text.

Checkpoint 1

How can posters on escalators be a positive influence on presentation work?

Take note

Numbers and other data forms are more difficult to read if underlined; space increases readability.

Checkpoint 2

Should a key point be in a contrasting or complementing colour to the background?

Don't forget

Poorly displayed or presented data not only slows down the information uptake but costs money in the form of time and mistakes.

A business hoping to attract investors needs to produce a well-planned presentation in a comfortable environment, making use of screen projectors to display computer-generated slides. This will impress an audience of potential investors better than hand-drawn diagrams on flip-chart presentations in a shabby uncomfortable room. A slick, fast moving presentation, emphasising confidence in the company's prospects would also help. A charity on the other hand may need to try a different approach in order to raise money for a good cause. People might shy away from a hi-tech presentation because they could perceive that the intended audience would be alienated by it.

Generally speaking clear well-spaced text or numbers on an uncluttered background are the easiest to follow. Graphs and data need to be clear and easy to follow. Tint and graduated background may look good but are not always the best backgrounds if you simply want to get a message across. Designers are expensive but often make the task of presenting information to the intended viewer, more efficient.

Technical Presentations

Many businesses need to produce presentations to their shareholders or clients. These need to be of a professional, high standard.

Over recent years a certain format has started to become adopted by many organisations, as a way of conveying information in a clear and interesting way.

All materials to be used in the presentation should have a corporate style – they must all use the same font, layout and colour scheme.

If a variety of materials are to be used, they must all be clearly identified, using clear titles and be referred to in a contents list.

If a multimedia presentation, such as PowerPoint is to be used, a paper version of the slides should be included in the pack – usually in multiple slide per page format.

Companies spend great amounts on developing a company 'look' to their materials, and have very strict guidelines on how their logos are used, or which fonts and typefaces can be used.

Checkpoint 3

Describe what a serif is.

Exam question   answer: pages 150–1

A mail order company has employed a web designer to redesign their web site, which the owner originally laid out (who has no design skills). They believe their products are good value but the web sales are poor. How could a professional designer help them increase sales?   (15 min)

Information and the professional

A job title is not always a reliable indication of the mechanics of a role. In order to help define what responsibilities belong to certain roles, codes of conduct were introduced, closely followed by codes of practice which outlined acceptable behaviour.

Check the net

An interesting web site providing the public and policy-makers with realistic assessments of the power, promise and problems of information technology is: www.cpsr.org

Checkpoint 1

Is the BCS a professional body?

The role of professional bodies

Professional bodies exist for many reasons – sometimes for prestige, sometimes to give like-minded individuals a common voice. These are some of the roles of professional bodies relating to ICT:

→ **Guidance** – both job-specific and behavioural. If an individual wishes to work in the field of ICT they may wish to meet certain standards, such as the hourly rate they might wish to charge for their services, or whether they should offer added services to the role they wish to supply, such as wiring as well as PC maintenance.
→ **Support** – forums exist for discussions regarding general and specific problems that individuals within the group face, and they may progress to action being taken on a member's behalf.
→ **To promote professional development and lifelong learning**, any profession needs to keep up with the times – it is important to all members that the opportunities exist for the members to improve their skills and knowledge.
→ **To add credibility to a profession and its members.** Although any individual is important, a group, with recognisable structures and spokespeople will often be taken more seriously.

Codes of conduct

These were originally introduced by professional bodies to help define roles and responsibilities attached to jobs in computing and ICT.

They can be seen in use in various organisations as non-disclosure agreements, i.e., during and after employment, you do not disclose any details of the organisation's business.

Codes of conduct are being built into contracts of employment more and more, so that employees know from the start:

→ What is acceptable or not.
→ What are their roles, responsibilities and levels of authority.
→ What the consequences of non-compliance are.

Take note

The nature of business competition in the information age makes the protection of proprietary information and computer networks an absolute necessity. Companies must have employees trained in information security to properly secure their computer networks and proprietary information.

Codes of practice

These define acceptable and some unacceptable practices (usually not exhaustive as this leads to 'creative' interpretation of what is unacceptable to make it appear acceptable). This could range from documenting software development in a certain manner through to selling systems to a customer.

Checkpoint 2

Why are 'codes of practice' useful ways of presenting a professional feeling to prospective customers?

They usually state that you should use your skills for the good of society, making it clear that members of the group will not carry out work that is unnecessary, or act in a manner that would cause offence or disgrace to the group or their customers. This would require a member to act in an honest and trustworthy manner.

It also requires that a member should not use pirated software/hardware (i.e., protected by copyright or patent) or ignore the intellectual property rights of developers who have yet to get their work protected by patent or copyright.

As a result of the rapid growth of computer networks, telecommunications networks and the Internet, a wealth of proprietary information and intellectual property is now stored on or transferred between computers. Information security is a rapidly developing field. More and more people will be required to develop an understanding of the scope and size of the issues involved in electronic cyber-crime, learn the value of setting policies, standards and procedures for the protection of information, and the importance of proper resource allocation, authority and support from the company executive to make the policies effective. Security tools such as a security audit and risk assessment will always need to be implemented and it is imperative to set up a computer network system based on sound security practices.

Ten points that companies should consider

1   Access control systems and methodology.
2   Application and systems development security.
3   Business continuity planning and disaster recovery planning.
4   Cryptography.
5   Law, investigation and ethics.
6   Operations security.
7   Physical security.
8   Security architecture and models.
9   Security management practices.
10 Telecommunications and networking security.

For each of these, the operatives need to be aware of the implications for themselves and their colleagues. This is where the role of professional bodies can be crucial, in forming policy and supporting their members in their work.

Many laws relating to ICT have come about through the pressure brought about by the professional bodies, such as the British Computer Society.

Checkpoint 3

Are roles and responsibilities of the supplier covered by a code of practice or conduct?

Take note

It is widely agreed that one of the greatest challenges facing corporations today is the security of their computer networks.

Exam question   answer: page 151

For what reasons do you think we need professional bodies?   (15 min)

Matching user requirements to the solution

The application of ICT solutions may not only result in minimisation of manpower, but it may also give management the chance to relocate or assign their staff to other productive and creative customer-relation building aspects of their business.

All projects need clear user requirements and a reliable way of tracing system requirements (and later, design elements and test requirements) back to them. Management facilities such as progress reports and status summaries can then be built on top of this structure.

The basic way to organise the user requirements is into three sections:

→ **Introduction** – a description of what is wanted.
→ **Functional requirements** – a list of what activities are wanted.
→ **Constraints** – a list of limitations or restrictions on the functions.

The list above is sometimes called 'textual description'.

Introduction

This is usually drawn up through discussion between the customer and supplier. Where possible a broad description of the expected outcome should be included. Obviously at this point there cannot be too much detail, but some pointers should be put forward.

The customer or client should be able to state their requirements, in broad terms, and the supplier should be able to offer some sort of outline solution.

Organising the functional requirements

There are many ways to group functions, all with their own advantages. A way that is effective and natural, and easy for users to grasp, is to organise them into scenarios.

A scenario is a time-ordered sequence of activities, forming an ideal or model use of the system being specified. Each activity will include one or several functions.

Emergency and other problem scenarios also need to be described. They may give rise to more functions (ways to get out of problems) or to constraints. For example, one scenario is that a car gets dented: a function that follows is repairing the car. This might result in specific design features later, such as quick repair systems (bolt-on wings).

Take note

User requirements should describe the problem to be solved; system requirements begin the whole process of solving that problem.

Checkpoint 1

What are the three sections of 'User requirements'?

Example

A simple way of setting up the basic structure of system requirements and traces is to use a tool to copy the functional and constraints sections of the user requirements document. This automatically creates links from each system requirement to the matching user requirement.

Checkpoint 2

How does organising functional requirements into 'scenarios' help to make the task of fulfilling the customer's needs easier?

In ICT terms a functional requirement may be that a user must be able to log on and print documents from a number of terminals in a particular centre. The scenario is straightforward, but the potential outcomes can range from relatively simple to extremely complicated. The actual outcome arrived at will depend upon a number of constraints.

Constraints ●●●

These may divide into sections, such as:

→ Performance.
→ Availability.
→ Safety.
→ Verifiability.
→ Maintainability.

Such categories often overlap.

Constraints may apply to the whole system, or just to a small part of it. For a constraint that applies to just one function, writing the constraint as an attribute can minimise effort. For a constraint that applies to several functions, it is undesirable to copy the constraint into each function, so the constraint text (or value) should be written down once, and its relationships indicated. This can be done in a database or requirements tool by linking the constraint to the functions to which it applies. The complexity of the task of creating and maintaining links is a good reason for using a software tool.

To go back to the printing scenario mentioned above, the performance of the system would be a major constraint. Users could have discrete profiles that load printer drivers onto the machine they log on to, or each machine could have the drivers installed beforehand.

For each of the constraints there will be a range of permissible outcomes. These can then be considered for the functional requirements and a possible solution put forward to the client.

Take note

System requirements should never simply be a copy of the user requirements. System requirements define what the system must do to satisfy user requirements, which necessitates both a system viewpoint, and complete traceability back to the user requirements document

Exam question answer: page 151

List the ways we could organise the user's requirements. (15 min)

Critical appraisal of information and

Checkpoint 1

Why is it important to ask 'is it still meeting its objectives?'

Take note

When considering all these issues the question for many organisations will be, 'Is ICT being managed?'

Many organisations use appraisal methods on ICT systems; usually they have little choice but to use ICT, e.g., those in the delivery and dependent sectors. Often the successful implementation of an ICT system depends on the co-operation of diverse groups who may have different views of how the system is to be used and thus it's usefulness.

Employee commitment is important, negative attitudes and poor training or involvement can lead to user resistance preventing the full potential of a system materialising. Office automation systems rely heavily on user support and commitment – user resistance can jeopardise system success.

All ICT investment proposals have to be appraised in terms of business needs. This will mean that the organisation should ask some general questions:

→ Will we use it?
→ How often will we use it?
→ What advantages will it give us?
→ Are the advantages positive and will they help the organisation to become more successful?

Following the introduction of a new system, the appraisal should take place, again, with a number of general questions to be answered:

→ Has the system met its objectives?
→ Is it still meeting those objectives?

A medium- to long-term investment in ICT systems needs continuous appraisal to assess the new and novel application of the system over time.

ICT systems that are introduced to increase the accuracy of information would be assessed using:

→ stages survey.
→ direct labour substitution.
→ cost–benefit analysis.

ICT systems introduced to increase staff productivity:

→ Porter's value chain analysis.

ICT systems that improve product quality or offer a better customer service:

→ customer lifecycle.
→ customer lock in, switching.

ICT systems that strategically exploit the potential of new technology:

→ risk analysis.
→ appraised by someone who understands the dynamics.

communications systems

There are various methods of appraising ICT systems:

→ Consider the technical costs.
→ Consider the human costs.
→ Consider the organisational costs.

Some of the more traditional methods of appraisal might be return on investment (ROI).

There is a move to use more risk analysis techniques to appraise ICT systems. Some possible techniques are Bayesion analysis, return on management, information economics and strategic contribution assessment.

Tangible and intangible benefits must be considered equally. Intangible benefits are not considered as important as tangible benefits when they often produce advantages that outweigh the original tangible benefits, e.g., e-mail systems intended for internal use adapted for customer contact.

Appraising costs ●●●

It is quite common to underestimate the support costs of many new systems.

→ Small but regular costs:
    → printers, upgrades, cables, disks, peripheral devices.
→ Environmental costs:
    → wiring, air conditioning, furniture and health and safety requirements.
→ Loss of business:
    → due to system failure.
    → software failure.
→ Higher wages for ICT staff:
    → installation costs of new equipment, teething problems.
→ Access fees to remote systems.
→ Time spent configuring software.
→ Time spent learning.
→ Time spent on evaluation.
→ Consultancy and training fees.
→ Customisation of packages.
→ Licence fees.

Checkpoint 2

Define the term 'customer lock-in'.

Example

Second order effects of ICT can also be far reaching, for instance, promoting work redesign and a fresh look at business processes and improvement. It can be used as a facilitator of organisational change.

Checkpoint 3

What is ROI and why is it important?

Exam question   answer: page 151

How would you go about appraising an ICT system? What would you be looking for?   (15 min)

Answers
Interaction

Human–computer interaction and interface

Checkpoints

1 Interpretation of end-user's requirements.
2 As computer costs fall, more people buy them, less experienced users therefore have access to more technologically advanced equipment.
3 Images can communicate actions or effects in a simpler form than text – therefore quicker to learn and understand.

Exam question

Employers should provide the following: ergonomically sound chairs and desks, up-lighting to reduce glare, position PCs away from windows unless blinds or tints are in place, provide wrist rests, ensure laser printers and copiers are placed away from the users. The position of the VDU or VDUs is probably the most important because the head, shoulders, back and eyes are all affected by bad positioning.

Design of the human–computer interface

Checkpoints

1 Jacquard.
2 Graphical user interface.
3 DOS requires typing instructions for actions, Windows-based systems use WIMP – allowing the user to point and click and letting the computer work out the procedure to carry out an action.

Exam question 1

The GUI system allows users to quickly carry out commands without having to program the DOS (disk operating system) in PCs. Prior to GUI PC users had to be fairly knowledgeable about DOS and learn to string command lines together in order for instance to delete a file, whereas today it is possible to simply move a picture of a file to a picture of a dustbin.

Exam question 2

Menu commands
- File – access to commands that relate to the general file commands – save, print, etc.
- Edit – commands to change data within the file such as copy/paste.
- View – control of the way the user sees the document.
- Insert – add data to a document, images, tables data from other applications.
- Format – layout and details for changing fonts, etc.
- Tools – co-operative working tools or procedures for checking work, spelling/grammar.
- Table – access to facilities that allow users to edit tables.
- Window – multiple views of different documents.
- Help – access to the help facilities.

User support and training

Checkpoints

1 A user guide is a concise set of instructions detailing how to do a particular thing, a manual covers all possible eventualities of using the equipment.
2 Computer-based training.
3 The company has to pay for the training, the employee is away from their normal role, so they are not being productive while they are training.

Exam question 1

Well-trained employees tend to be more efficient and confident about their work. Failure to train properly can lead to low morale and self-esteem eventually manifesting as low levels of motivation.

Larger companies and specialised companies who need skilled workers usually ensure that staff are well trained. Training however is expensive as the worker will not be productive while being trained, so this has to be viewed as a longer-term investment.

Exam question 2

One-to-one training is probably the quickest way to retrain staff but will be very expensive. Other ways of training include:
- Manuals and user booklets.
- Group tuition.
- Hand over training.
- Online context sensitive help (office assistant).
- Worked examples or tutorials as a learning tool.
- Magazines available in the High Street.
- Bulletin boards and user forums on the Internet.

Effective presentation of information and data

Checkpoints

1 Viewers get two or three seconds to take in the message from the poster – this is similar to viewers watching a presentation.
2 Contrasting colour to the background.
3 The small flicks on the ends of strokes used to form letters in a font.

Exam question

The designer should look at the presentation of tables and check whether or not they are easy to follow (the ordering process should be easy and simple to follow). This could include e-mail links and MS Word-based order forms.

The display of the goods should enable the viewer to make judgements fairly quickly. Therefore, the presentation of images needs to be clear, informative and present the product in the best possible light.

The overall presentation of the site should have something to do with the products on sale. The text should be sharp and readability should be excellent. The use of colour costs nothing on the web (printed matter increases in price with each colour). Finally the web offers designers the opportunity to create multi-media sites, with sound, animation and hyperlinks to provide an environment that helps sell a product.

Information and the professional

Checkpoints

1 Yes – the British Computer Society.
2 Customers know that a minimum level of service will be offered, at least, and that they can get similar services from a number of companies, that are bound to meet the customer's needs.
3 Practice.

Exam question

Professional bodies often reassure both members and the public, thus promoting confidence. For business they can act as a kind of rulebook.
- Guidance – both job-specific and behavioural.
- Support – forums exist for discussions.
- To promote professional development and lifelong learning.
- To add credibility to a profession and its members.

Matching user requirements to the solution

Checkpoints

1 Introduction, functional requirements, constraints.
2 Supplier and customer can walk through the scenario and ensure that all functions are there and appropriate.

Exam question

- Introduction (a description of what is wanted, what do we need?).
- Functional requirements (a list of what activities are wanted, what do we want it to do?).
- Constraints (a list of limitations or restrictions on the functions).

The list above is sometimes called 'textual description'.

Critical appraisal of information and communications systems

Checkpoints

1 Systems can appear to be doing what is required, when they are not – e-mail systems may be accepting spam e-mail, when a newer client would have a built-in filter, however the older system would still be carrying out the original task, when a newer system would be better at it.
2 Having a customer buy a product or service with some form of contract for further services, such as money back guarantee, or a service agreement that means they have to remain with the original supplier to avoid invalidating their warranty.
3 Return on investment, by putting money into a venture the stakeholder wants to get something in return, increased profits, or higher productivity.

Exam question

ICT systems need continuous appraisal to assess the new and novel application of the system over time.
You could ask the following questions:
- Are objectives met?
- Is this still happening?
- Does it improve product quality or offer a better customer service?
- Does it increase the accuracy of information, etc.?
- Does it increase staff productivity?
  Porter's value chain analysis
  customer lifecycle
  customer lock-in, switching.
- ICT systems that strategically exploit the potential of new technology.
  risk analysis
  appraised by someone who understands the dynamics.

Revision checklist
Interaction

By the end of this chapter you should be able to:

1	Understand and list the human/physical problems concerned with human interaction.	Confident	Not confident **Revise** page 136
2	Describe the use of icons.	Confident	Not confident **Revise** page 136
3	Have a clear understanding of the term developer support.	Confident	Not confident **Revise** page 140
4	List the various types of software training based on the trainees' needs.	Confident	Not confident **Revise** pages 140 and 141
5	Understand the use of training as a strategic consideration.	Confident	Not confident **Revise** page 141
6	Describe the reasons why effective presentation works.	Confident	Not confident **Revise** pages 142 and 143
7	Understand and list examples from the code of conduct.	Confident	Not confident **Revise** page 144
8	List the ten security points.	Confident	Not confident **Revise** page 145
9	Understand the role of professional bodies.	Confident	Not confident **Revise** page 144
10	Understand the basic way to organise the user requirements into three sections.	Confident	Not confident **Revise** pages 146 and 147
11	List the ways of organising functional requirements.	Confident	Not confident **Revise** pages 146 and 147
12	Make a list of constraints that apply to whole or part systems.	Confident	Not confident **Revise** page 147
13	Know what questions we should ask in an ICT appraisal.	Confident	Not confident **Revise** page 148

Resources

AS/A Level Information Technology is designed to give you some insight into ICT as a career. It builds up both theoretical and skill-based knowledge. The skillbase is tested and evidenced through the coursework elements of the course, and the theory through written papers (although, of course, both parts are tested to some extent by both methods). The examiner is not that interested in your ability to recall generic facts as they assume you are capable of doing this already. They are, however, very interested in your ability to read solutions into problems expressed as scenarios.

This last section of the book includes the following:

→ Revision techniques

→ Reading and note making

→ Answering exam questions

→ Glossary

Revision techniques

Check the net

There are hundreds of revision sites on the Internet. Be careful that you use UK-based sites, as many educational sites are American – there is a very different education system over there!

By this stage in your academic career, you will have studied for and passed many exams. Still, you may feel that some advice regarding methods of effective revision is worthwhile.

Notes

The best investment you can make is the time and effort it takes to produce high-quality notes. These notes will be the scaffolding that you use to support your knowledge. Some tips on making effective notes can be found in the section entitled, Reading and note making (page 156).

Once made, you must revisit your notes on a regular basis, mainly to train your memory how to react to your key words in the notes and recall the fine topic details as quickly as possible and also to ensure your notes are a true reflection of your current knowledge by adding new information to them, as required.

Past papers

Past papers will, hopefully, be a favoured method of organised revision sessions in class. Practising past papers gives you the best idea of how to time yourself on the day. Do try to treat past papers as the real thing, not some type of competition to see how quickly you can finish!

Compare these past papers with the mark schemes supplied by the examiner to the marker of the paper. Your teacher will be able to supply these – many can be sourced free on the Internet. Mark schemes do try to cover all possible answers but do not claim to be exhaustive. If, as a result of completing a past paper, you find that you have slightly different answers to those suggested, why not use the opportunity to discuss and debate your (sensible) answers with your peers and teachers?

Course syllabus

Syllabi are the starting point for your teachers when deciding which topics you are to study, so if they are good enough for them, they surely must be good enough for you! Why not use them as checklists to judge how much you know and more importantly to highlight what you don't know.

Cynical though it may be, you are examined on your ability to relate your knowledge only to the topics that have been chosen for inclusion in a syllabus – peripheral knowledge can, however, reinforce the impression that a good student makes on the examiner by showing that they have absorbed not only the syllabus, but have a pool of related knowledge from which to draw.

Examiner's secrets

Cramming the night before the examination can help, but it is not as successful as a structured revision programme. The exam will cover a whole year's work – trying to do it all in one night is bound to be less efficient.

Glossaries

If you find it difficult to recall the meanings of some of the technical jargon that you encounter on your ICT course, you may find it useful to compile a glossary of terms for your own use. The best way that we can recommend you do this is by taking terms and finding definitions for them from say a minimum of three sources. You then need to 'translate' the definitions into your own words. Keep building up this glossary until you have a sound collection that you are able to depend on less and less as your use of the terminology and confidence in your understanding of the meaning grows.

Cards ●●●

Making your notes and then condensing them is a valuable way to prepare yourself for examinations. It sometimes helps if you have access to these notes and the best way we have found is by transferring them, topic by topic onto A6 sized cards. This way, you can keep each of your topics separate and you can keep the cards handy so they can be referred to, as you need them, not when you get home, have fed the cat, done a hundred other things and then finally remembered that there is something that you can't remember!

On a smaller, yet quirkier scale, sticky notes placed around your room and other areas in your home may help as impromptu *aide memoires* in the days and weeks leading up to the examinations.

Fun ways ●●●

OK, so there aren't really any fun ways to revise for these extremely important exams but why not try to at least start a revision session with your peers in a fun way? You can make 'trivial pursuit' style cards covering various topics, e.g., communications and networking – devices, topologies, etc., legal aspects – DPA 8 principles, etc., and then 'play' a game, discussing any discrepancies or points of interest that may arise along the way. You could also 'play' ICT hangman, where the hangman thinks of a topic that will be the revision topic for the next 10 minutes.

Coping ●●●

A couple of tips from some people who have been there and done that:

→ Revision is best done in short bursts with pre-planned breaks along the way.
→ When you have completed reading a passage of text, try to summarise the content.
→ If you are tired, you will only end up distressing yourself that you have learned nothing – your brain is just telling you to shut the books and get some rest – be that 10 minutes and a cuppa or a decent night's sleep.
→ Make a clear timetable of exam dates and venues – it will help with last minute panics.

Reading and note making

Check the net

BBC do various revision support systems, bitesize is one of the most popular. Even though many of the revision sites are GCSE based, you may still find some very useful bits and pieces.

Check the net

BSC student membership details can be found at: www.bcs.org.uk

Watch out!

Examination boards are now called awarding bodies, and a syllabus is now called a specification.

Students of ICT are at a slight disadvantage to their peers in other subjects. Their subject material is constantly changing and therefore requires a good deal of *ad hoc* research. Making notes on the material found is as important as keeping up to date. Notes should be concise, yet retain clear meaning so that you know what the notes are about two to three weeks or six months later – whenever the topic is revised.

Sources of information

Textbooks
Specifically written for courses of study involving ICT. A-level specific ones may follow the syllabus closely. GNVQ or HND ones will act as sources of information to build up your knowledge base.

Magazines
Many ICT specific publications exist. The following are just some examples:

→ The *Computer Bulletin* – BCS members' magazine. See if your teacher or any ICT support staff have this as it covers many topics and specialises in the professional side of ICT, codes of practice, ethics, professional development, etc. (monthly).
→ *Computing* – general ICT interest magazine which gives insight to careers and roles (weekly).
→ *LAN* – networking and communications magazine (monthly).
→ *Computer Weekly*, *Computer telephony* and *ICT training* are examples of other, less-well-known magazines, again covering a range of topics.

The Internet
Many sites with discussion forums, research, definitions, future proposals, etc. – select a search engine and surf!

Newspaper supplements

→ *Connected* – free with the *Daily Telegraph* on Thursdays.
→ *Interface* – free with the *Guardian* on Wednesdays.

Check your school and local library for copies.

Syllabi
Close reading of the syllabus for your course will not only give you exactly what needs to be covered, but is usually expanded to give details about the types of sub-topics that will need to be investigated. Here are some addresses:

AQA (Assessment and Qualifications Alliance) for NEAB publications department, Stag Hill House, Guildford, Surrey, GU2 5XJ

Edexcel Foundation
Stewart House, 32 Russell Square, London, WC1B 5DN

OCR (Oxford, Cambridge and Royal Society of Arts)
1 Regent Street, Cambridge, CB2 1GG

Extracting relevant information

Not all the sources of information that you discover need to be read thoroughly in order to be of use to you. The depth of reading required will depend on the purpose of the information. With books, start at the back and take a look through the index. This should give you an idea of the topics covered. It is also worth looking at the contents page to reinforce the range of topics covered.

Quick skim reading

Quickly looking over a page or chapter will enable you to filter through large amounts of data in order to decide whether or not it deserves a second look.

Information search

Looking for specific information can be difficult as many peripheral topics may cross your path, tempting you off course. Having a clear idea of what topic you are information searching for will help. *Do not* rely on one source alone, especially if gained via the Internet, as there is no guarantee of it being valid. Instead, look at a few sources and check their consistency. This method will help you to understand researched information when presented in slightly different ways and check its correctness.

Building understanding

The term 'reading around a subject' refers to both casual and in-depth research that is undertaken by the serious student. It does not necessarily mean 'reading' but covers all methods of extending your subject knowledge, e.g., watching ICT-related TV programmes, discussing the Information Society with colleagues, absorbing the contents of ICT-related advertising, taking your computer apart to see how the components actually fit together, etc.

Check the net

Be careful – the Internet is not always right, so check your sources. Books usually get checked carefully by editors, and others, but pages can be put on the Internet without any checks!

Watch out!

The authors do not accept any liability for the consequences of the final suggestion – keep your motherboard manual handy!

Answering exam questions

AS and A Level ICT exam questions are written with four specific outcomes in mind. They will all test your ability to recall and display understanding, some will question your knowledge and others will question your ability to reason. The techniques for dealing with them are equally important and they demand your attention.

Question types ●●●

The four types of question are ones requiring:

→ Short, concise answers.
→ Structured answers showing progression in thought.
→ Synoptic evidence of your knowledge.
→ Extended answers.

Short, concise answers ●●●

These, generally, come about as a result of a short, concise question! They will use certain key words in their questioning:

→ *What* does WYSIWYG stand for?
→ *Define* the term 'firewall'.
→ *Explain* what is meant by validation.
→ *State* a benefit of using e-mail over snailmail.
→ *Give* two differences between a LAN and a WAN.

Structured answers showing progression in thought ●●●

Questions of this nature look for a commitment from you. The reply given for the first section may well have you tied into developing your answer further so *make sure* you read the whole question before writing down the first thing that comes into your head – you may not be able to keep up the momentum for the second, third or maybe fourth part of the question.

Maybe you'll be faced with:

'A computer system operates using pseudo real-time.'
 (i) *Define* the term pseudo real-time.
 (ii) *Outline* a scenario where the use of a pseudo real-time system is vital, explaining why it is needed.

Or it could be:

'DBMS have the ability to query the content of a database and extract reports of information.'
 (i) *Name* two common methods used to set up a query.
 (ii) *State* one advantage and one disadvantage of both of the methods named in part (i).

A question that has more than one part will only offer marks for an answer once – don't repeat answers.

Don't leave blank spaces, plan your time and try to answer every question.

Synoptic evidence of your knowledge ●●●

This is where you get to write what you know about something. Some examinations work with pre-release materials. You are expected to carry out some research about an agreed area, then write this up in the examination. With ICT examinations it is more likely to take the form of a topic you have studied during the course being used as the basis of a number of questions, one of which will expect a long answer.

Extended answers ●●●

These are questions that require you to put together an essay, usually discussing two viewpoints, or advantages and disadvantages. It may help to start by drawing up a table of the good and bad points, then using them as the basis for your essay.

Examination tips ●●●

→ Look at the *marks* available for each question. Two-mark questions require no more than a couple of sentences. Make sure, though, that you *do write in sentences*.

→ Avoid at all costs these phrases: *cheaper*, *faster* and more *efficient* without *explanation*.

→ *Full marks* for a question are *not possible* unless you give *relevant examples* whether you are asked to do this or not.

→ ICT must be seen in its *wider* sense – financial systems, report generation, business systems.

→ Avoid *standard* answers committed to memory. So easy to spot!

→ Avoid *colloquialisms* and *slang*.

→ *Hardware* related answers must *relate* to the way in which *organisations work*.

→ *Never rewrite* answers from earlier questions in the vain hope of gaining marks for another question.

Essay answers ●●●

→ Use *sub headings* (from the question) but write in *sentences* and *paragraphs*.

→ Do not repeat yourself or use the advantage of one point as a disadvantage of another.

→ For *20-mark* questions *usually*:
  → Grammar, spelling and punctuation are worth 1 mark.
  → Clarity of expression and use of technical language – (1)
  → Structure – (1)
  → Presentation and development of ideas – (1)

→ Spend a couple of minutes *planning* this type of answer and *don't* answer it *last*.

Check the net

Make sure you are clear about the expectations of the examination board:
www.ocr.org.uk
www.aqa.org.uk
www.edexcel.org.uk

Watch out!

Examinations do not cover the whole of the syllabus each year; don't just expect to get asked the same questions year after year.

Glossary

Access provider

The company that gives you Internet access.

Acoustic coupler

A modem, which converts digital signals into sound for transmission through telephone lines, and performs the reverse operation when receiving such signals. Acoustic couplers generally have cups for the telephone handset.

Active window

The top or front window in a multiple window environment.

A/D converter

A device used to convert analogue data to digital data. Analogue data is continuously variable, while digital data contains discrete steps.

Address resolution

Conversion of an IP address to the corresponding low-level physical address.

A-drive

The drive that the floppy disk uses, not used very much these days as files are often too large to fit.

AIX

Advanced interactive executive – IBM's version of Unix.

Aliasing

Visibly jagged steps along angled or object edges, due to sharp tonal contrasts between pixels.

Analogue

Continuously variable signals or data.

Anonymous login convention (FTP)

Standard username (*anonymous*) and password (*guest*), *which* allows login within FTP for the purpose of retrieving an unprotected file.

Application

Software that lets users do relatively complex tasks, as well as create and modify documents. Common application types include word processors, spreadsheets, database managers, and presentation graphics programs.

ARP

Address resolution protocol. Used to dynamically discover the low-level physical network hardware address that corresponds to the high level IP address for a given host, for instance. ARP is limited to physical network systems that support broadcast packets that can be heard by all hosts on the network.

ASCII

American (national) standard code for information interchange. A standard character-to-number encoding widely used in the computer industry.

Associate

Linking a document with the program that created it so that both can be opened with a single command.

AU sounds

A type of audio format used in the World Wide Web.

AV

Audio-visual. Video-capture hardware and has sophisticated sound (and video) recording capabilities.

Backbone

Network used to interconnect several networks together.

Backup file

A compressed version of the original file and its locations created by Backup.

Bandwidth

The capacity of the transmission medium stated in bits per second or as a frequency. The bandwidth of optical fibre is in the gigabit or billion bits per second range, while Ethernet coaxial cable is in the megabit or million bits per second range.

Baseband system

A baseband system transmits signals without converting them to another frequency and is characterised by its support of one frequency of signals. Ethernet-based networks inside campus buildings are transmitted via baseband coaxial cable, with ethernet being the only service supported by the coaxial cable.

BAT

Filename extension for a batch file.

Batch scanning

Sequential scanning of multiple originals using previously defined, unique settings for each.

Baud

A unit of measurement that denotes the number of bits that can be transmitted per second. For example, if a modem is rated at 9,600 baud it is capable of transmitting data at a rate of 9,600 bits per second. The term was derived from the name of JME Baudot, a French pioneer in the field of printing telegraphy.

BBS

Bulletin board service. A non commercial dial-up service usually run by a user group or software company. By dialling up a BBS with your modem, you can exchange messages with other users, and upload or download software.

BGI

Binary gateway interface. Provides a method of running a program from a web server. Similar to a common gateway interface (CGI). The BGI uses a binary dynamic link library (DLL) which is loaded into memory when the server starts. While more efficient than a CGI, the BGI must be compiled and is not easily portable to other environments.

Bilevel

A type of image containing only black and white pixels.

Binary

A numbering system with only two values: 0 (zero) and 1 (one).

Binary file

A file that contains more than plain text (i.e., photos, sounds, spreadsheet, etc.). In contrast to an ASCII file which only contains plain text.

Binary number system

A counting system used in computers consisting of only 1s and 0s (zeros).

BinHex

A file conversion format that converts binary files to ASCII test files.

BIOS

Basic input–output system. Part of the computer's operating system that is built into the machine, rather than read from a disk drive at startup.

Bit

A unit of measurement that represents one figure or character of data. A bit is the smallest unit of storage in a computer. Since computers actually read 0s and 1s, each is measured as a bit. The letter *A* consists of 8 bits which amounts to one byte. Bits are often used to measure the capability of a microprocessor to process data, such as 16-bit or 32-bit.

Bit depth

The number of bits used to represent each pixel in an image, determining its colour or tonal range.

Bit-map

Generally used to describe an illustration or font file as being created by a predefined number of pixels. *See also* **object-oriented**.

Black point

A movable reference point that defines the darkest area in an image, causing all other areas to be adjusted accordingly.

Booting

Starting up a computer via the power switch, which loads the system software into memory. Restarting the computer via a keystroke combination is called rebooting or a warm boot.

bps

Bits per second is the unit used for measuring line speed, the number of information units transmitted per second.

Bridge

A dedicated computer used to connect two different networks. It uses data link layer address (i.e., ethernet physical addresses) to determine if packets should be passed between the networks.

Broadband system

A broadband system is capable of transmitting many different signals at the same time without interfering with one another. For local area networks, a broadband system is one that handles multiple channels of local area network signals distributed over cable television (CATV) hardware.

Broadcast

A packet whose special address results in its being heard by all hosts on a computer network.

Browser

A program that enables you to access information on the Internet through the World Wide Web.

Bug

A mistake, or unexpected occurrence, in a piece of software or in a piece of hardware.

Byte

The amount of memory needed to store one character such as a letter or a number. Equal to 8 bits of digital information. The standard measurement unit of a file size.

Cache

An area of RAM reserved for data recently read from disk, which allows the processor to quickly retrieve it if it's needed again.

Caching

A process in which frequently accessed data is kept on hand, rather than constantly being retrieved from the place where it is stored.

Case-dependent

Software differentiation between upper- and lower-case characters. Also referred to as case sensitive.

CCD

Charge-coupled device. An integrated, micro-electrical light sensing device built into some image-capturing devices.

CD-ROM

Compact disk, read-only memory. A type of storage device that looks just like an audio CD and stores as much data as a large hard disk (600 MB), making it a popular means of distributing fonts, photos, electronic encyclopaedias, games, and multi-media offerings. As the name indicates, however, you can't save or change files on a CD-ROM, only read them. Pronounced *see-dee rom*.

CGI

Common gateway interface. A method of running an executable script or program from a web server. When a client requests a URL pointing to a CGI, the program is run and the results are returned to the client. This enables dynamic web pages and the ability to do database queries and other complex operations across the web.

Circuit-switched

A type of network connection which establishes a continuous electrical connection between calling and called users for their exclusive use until the connection is released. Ericsson PBX is a circuit-switched network.

Clickable image

Any image that has instructions embedded in it so that clicking on it initiates some kind of action or result. On a web page, a clickable image is any image that has a URL embedded in it.

Client/server relationship

A client application is one that resides on a user's computer, but sends requests to a remote system to execute a designated procedure using arguments supplied by the user. The computer that initiates the request is the client and the computer responding to the request is the server. Many network services follow a client and server protocol.

Clipboard

An area used to temporarily store cut or copied information. The clipboard can store text, graphics, objects and other data. The clipboard contents are erased when new information is placed on the clipboard or when the computer is shut down.

Clipping

The conversion of all tones lighter than a specified grey level to white, or darker than a specified grey level to black, causing loss of detail. This also applies to individual channels in a colour image.

CMS

Colour management system. This ensures colour uniformity across input and output devices so that final printed results match originals. The characteristics or profiles of devices are normally established by reference to standard colour targets.

CMYK

Cyan, magenta, yellow and black are the base colours used in printing processes. CMY are the primary colourants of the subtractive colour model.

Coaxial cable

A type of cable that contains two conductors. The central conductor is surrounded by a layer of insulation, which is then wrapped by a braided-metal conductor and an outer layer of insulation.

Colorimeter

A light-sensitive device for measuring colours by filtering their red, green and blue components, as in the human eye. *See also* **spectrophotometer**.

Colour cast

An overall colour imbalance in an image, as if viewed through a coloured filter.

COM1, COM2, etc.

Most serial ports and internal modems on DOS/WIN PCs can be configured to either COM1 or COM2 in order to accommodate the situation where both may exist. The DOS MODE command is used to change the output direction to such serial devices as modems.

Compression

The reduction in size of an image file. *See also* **non-lossy**.

Configuration

(1) The components that make up a computer system (which model and what peripherals).
(2) The physical arrangement of those components (what's placed and where).
(3) The software settings that enable two computer components to talk to each other (as in configuring communications software to work with a modem).

Contone (CT)

An abbreviation for continuous tone. A colour or greyscale image format capable of illustrating continuously varying tonal ranges, as opposed to line art.

Cookies

A file sent to a web browser by a web server that is used to record once's activities.

Coprocessor

A chip designed specifically to handle a particular task, such as maths calculations or displaying graphics on-screen. A coprocessor is faster at its specialised function than the main processor is, and it relieves the processor of some work. A coprocessor can reside on the motherboard or be part of an expansion card, as with an accelerator.

CPU

Central processing unit: the brains of the computer. The CPU interprets and executes the actual computing tasks.

Crash

A problem (often caused by a bug) that causes a program, or the entire operating system, to unexpectedly stop working.

Cross-platform

Refers to software (or anything else) that will work on more that one platform (type of computer).

Cursor

The representation of the mouse on the screen. It may take many different shapes. Example: I-beam, arrow pointer and hand.

Cyberspace

A term used to refer to the electronic universe of information available through the Internet.

DAT

Digital audio tape. The most common type of tape backup.

Database

A file created by a database manager that contains a collection of information organised into records, each of which contains labelled categories (called fields).

Daughterboard

A board that attaches to (rides piggyback on) another board, such as the motherboard or an expansion card. For example, you can often add a daughterboard containing additional memory to an accelerator card.

DCS

Desktop colour separation. An image format consisting of four separate CMYK PostScript files at full resolution, together with a fifth EPS master for placement in documents.

Decompression

The expansion of compressed image files. *See also* **non-lossy**.

Dedicated line

A telephone or data line that is always available. For example, a leased telephone line can be dedicated for computer data communications. This line is not used by other computers or individuals, is available 24 hours a day, and is never disconnected.

Default route

A routing table entry which is used to direct packets addressed to networks not explicitly listed in the routing table.

Densitometer

A measuring instrument that registers the density of transparent or reflective materials. Colours are read as tonal information. *See also* **colorimeter** and **spectrophotometer**.

Density

Density is a brightness control to lighten or darken a printout to more closely reflect its screen appearance and to compensate for deficiencies in toner or paper quality.

Descreening

Removal of halftone dot patterns during or after scanning printed matter by defocusing the image. This avoids moiré patterning and colour shifts during subsequent halftone reprinting.

Dialog box

A window that displays additional options or questions when a command is chosen.

Dial-up line

A communication connection from your computer to a host computer over standard phone lines. Unlike a dedicated line, you must dial the host computer in order to establish a connection. Dial-up line is currently the most popular form of net connection for the home user.

Dichroic mirror

A special type of interference filter, which reflects a specific part of the spectrum, while transmitting the rest. Used in scanners to split a beam of light into RGB components.

Digital

Data or voltages consisting of discrete steps or levels, as opposed to continuously variable analogue data.

Digitisers

A machine which converts analogue data into digital data on a computer (such as a scanner digitising pictures or text).

DIP switches

Dual interface poll switches allow for either an *on* or *off* setting with any number of circuits. DIP switches commonly allow you to change the configuration of a circuit board to suit your particular computer.

Direct connection

A permanent communication connection between your computer system (either a single CPU or a LAN) and the Internet. This is also called a leased line connection because you are leasing the telephone connection from the phone company. A direct connection is in contrast to a SLIP/PPP or dial-up connection.

Direct-to-plate

Direct exposure of image data onto printing plates, without the intermediate use of film.

Direct-to-press

Elimination of intermediate film and printing plates by the direct transfer of image data to printing cylinders in the press.

Directory

A system that your computer uses to organise files on the basis of specific information.

Disk defragmenter

Arranges the blocks of information for a file into adjacent blocks on your hard drive, which may significantly improve the file access times.

Dmax

The point of maximum density in an image or an original.

Dmin

The point of minimum density in an image or an original.

Domain name server

A computer that converts host names, such as rohan.sdsu.edu to its corresponding IP address, such as 191.130.1.10. In this instance, a San Diego State University computer provides this service any time mail is sent or received and permits users to use TELNET and FTP between SDSU and other sites.

DOS

Disk operating system. The operating system used on IBM personal computers and compatible machines.

Dotted decimal notation

The convention for writing 32-bit IP addresses as a set of four 8-bit numbers written in base 10 with periods separating them.

Down-sampling

The reduction in resolution of an image, necessitating a loss in detail.

Download

To retrieve a file from another computer using a modem.

dpi

Dots per inch. A measure of the resolution of a printer, scanner or monitor. It refers to the number of dots in a one-inch line. The more dots per inch, the higher the resolution.

Driver

A piece of software that tells the computer how to operate an external device, such as a printer, hard disk, CD-ROM drive or scanner. For instance, you can't print unless you have a printer driver. Hard disk drivers are invisible files that are loaded into memory when you start the computer, while scanner drivers are usually plug-ins accessed from within a particular application.

Drum scanner

Early drum scanners separated scans into CMYK data, recording these directly onto film held on a second rotating drum.

DTP

Desktop publishing.

Dump

Backup of data.

Duplex (full, half)

Full duplex is data flowing in both directions at the same time. When remote echo is *on* communication is occurring in full duplex. Half duplex has data moving in only one direction at a time (local echo is *on*).

DXF

Drawing interchange format used for Macintosh graphic files. The standard file-exchange format for 3-D and CAD programs.

Dye sublimation

A printing process using small heating elements to evaporate pigments from a carrier film, depositing these smoothly onto a substrata.

Echo (local, remote)

Local echo *on* causes all transmitted data to be sent to the screen of the sending computer. Remote echo *on* causes everything that the remote computer (the one you are communicating with) transmits to be duplicated on your computer's screen. *See* **Duplex**.

E-mail

Electronic mail. Private messages sent between users on different computers, either over a network or via a modem connection to an online service or BBS.

Encoding

File transfer formatting that enables encrypted, compressed or binary files to be transferred without corruption or loss of data.

Encryption

A way of coding information in a file or e-mail message so that if it is intercepted by a third party as it travels over a network it cannot be read.

EPS

Encapsulated PostScript. An EPS file usually has two parts: a PostScript (text) description that tells a PostScript printer how to output the resolution-independent image, and (optionally) a bit-mapped PICT image for on-screen previews (EPS files without a PICT preview is usually displayed as a grey rectangle). EPS files generally can't be edited, even by the program that created them (illustrator files are exceptions).

Ethernet

An IEEE 802.3 standard data-link layer which can operate over several different media including fibre-optic, coaxial cable and twisted-pair cable. This 10 million-bit-per-second networking scheme is widely used on campus because it can network a wide variety of computers; it is not proprietary; and components are widely available from many commercial sources.

Executable file

Refers to a file that is a program. Executables in DOS and Windows usually have an .exe or a .com extension. In UNIX and Macintosh environments, executable files can have any name.

External viewer

Program used for presenting graphics, audio and movies while browsing World Wide Web pages via a web client program. Helper applications is another term for these external programs.

FAQ

Frequently asked questions. A document that covers a topic of general concern to many users. FAQs are a good way for new users to get information on various aspects of the Internet.

File

A collection of information on a disk, usually a document or a program, that's lumped together and called by one name.

File permissions

When you place files on a UNIX system you can assign the files various levels of permission, specifying who can access them, and what type of access they can have.

File server

A computer that shares its resources, such as printers and files, with other computers on the network. An example of this is a Novell NetWare Server which shares its disk space with a workstation that does not have a disk drive of its own.

Film recorder

Used in reference to colour transparency recording devices, and sometimes also to imagesetters.

Filter

A piece of software that an application uses for file-format conversion or special effects. PageMaker, for example, has a filter that lets it import Microsoft Word files, while Photoshop has dozens of filters for special effects (such as image blurring). Filters can be part of the main application or external programs called plug-ins.

Finger

A program that displays information about someone on the Internet.

Firewall

A mechanism that isolates a network from the rest of the Internet, permitting only specific traffic to pass in and out.

Flatbed scanner

Any scanning device that incorporates a flat transparent plate, on which original images are placed for scanning. The scanning process is linear rather than rotational.

Floating-point processor

A special chip that handles sophisticated calculations, such as those used in spreadsheets, CAD and scientific programs.

Folder

An object that can hold other objects, such as other folders and files.

Font

The software that creates a typeface on a computer screen.

Format

To initialise a disk to prepare it for use. The disk is checked for errors and organised so that data can be recorded and retrieved. Formatting a used disk erases any previously stored information.

FPO

For position only. A low-resolution image placed in a document to indicate where the final version is to be positioned.

Fragmentation

A condition where parts of a file are stored in different locations on a disk. When a file is fragmented, the drive's read/write head has to jump from place to place to read the data; if many files are fragmented, it can slow the drive's performance.

Frame-grabbing system

A combination of hardware and software, designed to capture individual frames from video clips for further digital manipulation, or consecutive replay on computer platforms.

FTP

File transfer protocol. The Internet standard high-level protocol for transferring files from one computer to another across the network.

FTP site

A computer which stores files that can be retrieved using FTP. FTP sites which allow anyone to retrieve files (without having an account on that computer) are known as anonymous FTP sites.

Gamma correction

The correction of tonal ranges in an image, normally by the adjustment of tone curves.

Gamut

The limited range of colours provided by a specific input device, output device or pigment set.

Gang scanning

Sequential scanning of multiple originals using the same previously defined exposure setting for each.

Gateway

A special-purpose dedicated computer that attaches to two or more disparate networks and converts data packets from one form to another.

Gb

Gigabit. 10^9 bits of information (usually used to express a data transfer rate; as in, 1 Gigabit/second = 1 Gbps).

GB

Gigabyte. A unit of data storage size which represents 10^9 (one billion) characters of information.

GCR (grey component replacement)

A technique for replacing all the neutral tones of an image with an appropriate amount of black.

GIF

Graphic interchange format (pronounced *jiff*). A file compression format developed by CompuServe for transferring graphic files to and from online services.

Gigabyte

1,024 megabytes, or 1,048,576 kilobytes of digital data.

Graphical user interface (GUI)

The graphical visual representation of the working environment that presents the elements of your computer as objects on a desktop.

Grey balance

The balance between CMY colourants required to produce neutral greys without a colour cast.

Grey levels

Discrete tonal steps in a continuous tone image, inherent to digital data. Most contone (CT) images will contain 256 grey levels per colour.

Greyscale

A continuous tone image comprising black, white and grey data only.

Hacker

Slang term for a technically sophisticated computer user who enjoys exploring computer systems and programs, sometimes to the point of obsession.

Halftone

A simulation of continuous tones by the use of black or overlapping process colour dots of varying size or position.

Halftoning factor

See **quality factor**.

Halo

A light line around object edges in an image, produced by the USM (sharpening) technique.

Handle

Unique character string identifier assigned to each entry in the Networked Information Center WHOIS database.

Handshaking

The process computers and modems go through in order to establish a connection and agree on the speed and protocols for data transmission.

Header

The portion of a packet, preceding the actual data, containing source and destination addresses, error checking and other fields. A header is also the part of an electronic mail message that precedes the body of a message and contains, among other things, the message originator, date and time.

High key

A light image that is intentionally lacking in shadow detail.

Highlight

The lightest tones in an image. A spectral highlight is a bright, reflected light source.

Histogram

A chart displaying the tonal ranges present in an image as a series of vertical bars.

Home page

The document that is displayed when you first open a web client program. Also, commonly used to refer to the first document you come to in a collection of documents on a web site.

Host

The main computer system to which users are connected.

Hostname

Name which officially identifies each computer attached to the Internet.

HP

Hewlett-Packard.

HTML

HyperText markup language. A system for tagging various parts of a web document that tells the web client programs how to display the document's text, links, graphics and attached media.

Hue

The colour of an object perceived by the eye due to the fact that a single or pair of RGB primary colours predominates.

Hypermedia

Describes hypertext in which various types of data can be stored – sound, images, video and so on – as regular text.

Hypertext

A text-linking strategy that lets you jump between related information in a document by clicking on a button or highlighted word. Online help systems often use hypertext links, as do some programs designed for the electronic distribution of documents.

I-beam

The blinking vertical line that shows the point at which text or graphics will be inserted.

IBM

International Business Machines Corporation.

Icon

A graphical symbol, usually representing a file, folder, disk or tool.

Image map

A graphic divided into regions or 'hotspots'. When a particular region is clicked, it calls up a web page that has been associated with that particular region.

Imagesetter

A device used to record digital data (images and text) onto monochrome film or offset litho printing plates by means of a single or multiple intermittent light beams. Colour separated data is recorded as a series of slightly overlapping spots to produce either solid areas of line-art or halftone dots for printing continuous tones.

Import

To bring data into a document from another document, often generated by a different application.

I/O

Input/output.

Inactive window

A window that is open but is not the top window.

Information technology

Includes matters concerned with the furtherance of computer science and technology, design, development, installation and implementation of information systems and applications.

Initialising (formatting)

Setting up a disk (any kind) to receive information. When a disk is initialised (formatted), its magnetic media is divided into tracks and sectors, and structure files that your computer uses to keep track of data are created.

Inline images

Graphics that are contained within a document's textual information. In a web document, these graphics can either be loaded automatically when the page is accessed or loaded manually by clicking on the image's icon.

Installer

A utility that copies system software or an application from floppy disks or a CD-ROM to your hard disk. An installer may also decompress the new files, remove obsolete files, place extensions and control panels in their proper folders, and/or create new folders.

Interface

The way a computer interacts with a user or a peripheral.

Internet

The Internet (note the capital **I**) is the largest Internet in the world. It is a three-level hierarchy composed of backbone networks (e.g., NSFNET, MILNET), mid-level networks, and stub networks. The Internet is a multiprotocol internet.

Interpolation

In the image manipulation context, this is the increase of image resolution by the addition of new pixels throughout the image, the colours of which are based on neighbouring pixels.

Interrupt

A brief interruption of the computer's activity so that an urgent task can be performed.

IP

Internet protocol is the standard that allows dissimilar hosts to connect to each other through the Internet. This protocol defines the IP datagram as the basic unit of information sent over the Internet. The IP datagram consists of an IP header followed by a message.

IP address

Network addresses are usually of two types: (1) the physical or hardware address of a network interface card; for Ethernet this 48-bit address might be 0260.8C00.7666. The hardware address is used to forward packets within a physical network; and (2) the logical or IP address is used to facilitate moving data between physical networks and is made up of a network number, a subnetwork number, and a host number. All Internet addresses at SDSU have a network number of 130.191, a subnet number in the range of 1–254, and a host number in the range of 1–254.

IP datagram

The basic unit of information passed across the Internet. An IP datagram is to the Internet as a hardware packet is to a physical network. It contains a source and destination address along with data. Large messages are broken down into a sequence of IP datagrams.

IRC

Internet relay chat. A program that allows you to carry on 'live' conversations with people all over the world by typing messages back and forth across the Internet.

ISAAC

Information system for advanced academic computing. Serves as a clearinghouse for information about the use of IBM-compatible hardware and software as aids to instruction and research in higher education. Membership is free to all students, faculty and staff at these institutions.

ISO

International Organisation for Standardisation, the group that developed the OSI protocols.

ISP

Internet service provider. A company that provides access to the Internet. A service provider can offer simple dial-up access, SLIP/PPP access, or a dedicated line.

Java

An object-oriented programming language to create executable content (i.e., self-running applications) that can be easily distributed through networks like the web.

JPEG

Joint photographic experts group is a graphic file format that has a sophisticated technique for compressing full-colour bit-mapped graphics, such as photographs.

Kb

Kilobit. 10^3 bits of information (usually used to express a data transfer rate; as in, 1 Kilobit/second = 1 Kbps = 1 Kb).

KB

KiloByte. A unit of data storage size which represents 10^3 (one thousand) characters of information.

Kernel size

The number of pixels sampled as a unit during image manipulation and sharpening processes.

Keyword

Specified words used in text search engines.

Kilobyte (KB)

1,024 bytes of digital data.

LAN

Local area network. A network of directly-connected machines (located in close proximity), providing high-speed communication over physical media such as fibre-optics, coaxial cable or twisted-pair wiring.

Laser printer

Although a number of devices employ laser technology to print images, this normally refers to black-and-white desktop printers, which use the dry toner, xerographic printing process.

Laserdisc

A 12-inch disk that's similar to an audio CD but holds visual images (such as high-quality movies) as well as music. Also called a videodisc.

Line art

Images containing only black and white pixels. Also known as bilevel images. The term line art is sometimes used to describe drawings containing flat colours without tonal variation.

Links

Synonymous with anchors, hotlinks and hyperlinks.

Local system

The system you are using. Interactions between your computer and another computer on the Internet are sometimes described using the terms 'local' and 'remote' systems. The local system is your computer and the remote system is the other computer.

Login

The account name used to access a computer system.

Low key

A dark image that is intentionally lacking in highlight detail.

LPI/LPCM

Lines per inch or per centimetre. Units of measurement for screen ruling.

Mail merge

The merging of database information (such as names and addresses) with a letter template in a word processor, in order to create personalised letters.

Mailing list

A list of e-mail users who are members of a group. A mailing list can be an informal group of people who share e-mail with one another, or it can be a more formal LISTSERV group which discusses a specific topic.

Mainframe

A large, multi-tasking computer that is used by many users.

Math coprocessor

Another name for a floating-point processor.

Matrix

This often refers to a 2-dimensional array of CCD elements.

Medium

The material used to support the transmission of data. Examples include twisted-pair wire, coaxial cable, optical fibre, or electromagnetic wave (microwave).

Megabit (Mb)

Megabit. 10^6 bits of information (usually used to express a data transfer rate; as in, 1 Megabit/second = 1 Mbps).

Megabyte (MB)

MegaByte. A unit of data storage size which represents 10^6 (one million) characters of information.

Megahertz (MHz)

A million cycles (occurrences, alterations, pulses) per second. Used to describe the speed at which a computer's processor (or CPU) operates.

Memory

In general, another word for dynamic RAM, the chips where the computers store system software, programs, and data you are currently using. Other kinds of computer memory you may encounter are parameter RAM (PRAM), video RAM (VRAM), and static RAM (SRAM). Most computer memory is volatile, that is, its contents are lost when the computer shuts down.

Menu

A list of commands.

Menu bar

The horizontal bar that contains the names of available menus. The menu bar is located below the title bar.

Message

A collection of data that is ordered according to the rules of a given protocol suite, such that it is intelligible to the sending and receiving software.

MHz

Megahertz. A million cycles (occurrences, alterations, pulses) per second. Used to describe the speed at which a computer's processor (or CPU) operates. A 25-MHz processor can handle 25 million operations per second.

MIDI

Musical instrument digital interface. A technology that enables a computer to record and play musical performance.

Midtone

The middle range of tones in an image.

MILNET

Military network. A network used for unclassified military production applications. It is part of the Defense Data Network and the Internet.

MIME mappings

A list of file extensions and the types of files they belong to. When the server sends an HTTP reply, it sends a type/subtype header according to the requested file's extension.

MIME type/subtype

A HyperText Transfer Protocol (HTTP) header sent with a reply that determines how a client will view or use the message. The MIME type tells the general type of document, such as image or application, and the subtype tells the specific type such as GIF or ZIP.

MIPS

Millions of instructions per second.

Mirror site

An FTP site that is created after the contents of an original FTP archive server are copied to it. Usually, mirror sites use larger and faster systems than the original, so it's easier to obtain material from the mirror. Mirror sites are usually updated daily, so everything on the original is also at the mirrors. Tip – always use the mirror site that is physically closest to you.

Modem

A device which converts digital signals into analogue signals (*and back*) for transmission over telephone lines (*modulator and demodulator*).

Moiré

A repetitive interference pattern caused by overlapping symmetrical grids of dots or lines having differing pitch or angle.

Monochrome

Single-coloured. An image or medium displaying only black-and-white or greyscale information. Greyscale information displayed in one colour is also monochrome.

Motherboard

The heart, soul and brains of a computer. This plastic board resembles a miniature city, but its buildings are actually chips for things like the processing, RAM and ROM, and the tiny roads connecting them are circuit traces. Also called the logic board. There are no fatherboards or sonboards, but *see* **daughterboard**.

MOV

A file extension found on the World Wide Web that denotes that the file is a movie or video in QuickTime format.

MPEG

Moving pictures expert group. MPEG is an international standard for video compression and desktop movie presentation. You need a special viewing application to run the MPEG movies on your computer. MPEG II is a newer standard for broadcast-quality video.

Multimedia

Any presentation or software program that combines several media, such as graphics, sound, video, animation and/or text.

Multiplex

The division of a single transmission medium into multiple logical channels supporting many apparently simultaneous sessions.

Multi-tasking

The capability of an operating system to handle multiple processing tasks, apparently, at the same time.

Native

Software that's written specifically to run on a particular processor. Also, the file format in which an application normally saves its documents. The native format is generally readable only by that application (other programs can sometimes translate it using filters).

Navigation tools

Allows users to find their way around a web site or multimedia presentation. They can be hypertext links, clickable buttons, icons, or image maps.

Netiquette

A form of online etiquette. This term refers to an informal code of conduct that governs what is generally considered to be the acceptable way for users to interact with one another online.

Netware

The high priest of network operating systems.

Network

In general, a group of computers set up to communicate with one another. Your network can be a small system that's physically connected by cables (a LAN), or you can connect separate networks together to form larger networks (called WANs). The Internet, for example, is made up of thousands of individual networks.

News

A term often used to denote USENET news, a popular forum for discussion on the Internet.

Newsgroup

A discussion group, usually found on USENET news. Each group devotes its discussions to a specific topic.

Newsreader

A software program that lets you subscribe to newsgroups as well as read and post messages to them.

Node

A computer that is attached to a network; sometimes called a host.

Noise

In the scanning context, this refers to random, incorrectly read pixel values, normally due to electrical interference or device instability.

Non-lossy

Image compression without loss of quality.

Object-oriented

Generally used to describe an illustration or font file as being created by mathematical equations. *See also* **bit-map**.

OCR

Optical character recognition. A technology that lets you scan a printed page (with a scanner) and convert it into a text document that you can edit in a word processor.

Offset lithography

A high-volume, ink-based printing process, in which ink adhering to image areas of a lithographic plate is transferred (offset) to a blanket cylinder before being applied to paper or other substrate.

Online

Actively connected to other computers or devices. You're online when you've logged on to a network, BBS, or online service. A device such as a printer is online when it's turned on and accessible to a computer. If you're not online then you're offline.

Online service

A commercial service that (for a price) provides goodies such as e-mail, discussion forums, technical support, software libraries, news, weather reports, stock prices, plane reservations, even electronic shopping malls. To access one, you need a modem. Popular online services include America Online, CompuServe and Prodigy.

Operating system

Software that supervises and controls tasks on a computer.

Optical resolution

In the scanning context, this refers to the number of truly separate readings taken from an original within a given distance, as opposed to the subsequent increase in resolution (but not detail) created by software interpolation.

Optical video disc

Compact discs which use lights to read information.

OSI

Open systems interconnection. A set of standard protocols grouped into seven layers: the physical, data link, network, transport, session, presentation, and application layers.

Packet

The unit of data sent across a packet-switching network. While some Internet literature uses the term to refer specifically to data sent across a physical network, other literature views the Internet as a packet-switching network and describes IP datagrams as packets.

Packet-switching

Data transmission process, utilising addressed packets, whereby a channel is occupied only for the duration of the packet transmission. SDSUnet is a packet-switching network.

Parallel cable/parallel port

A cable used to connect peripheral devices through a computer's parallel port. A type of port that transmits data in parallel (several bits side by side).

Parameter

A word, number, or symbol that is typed after a command to further specify how the command should function.

Parity

A check bit used to make the sum of the bits in a unit of data either even or odd (including the parity bit). A unit of data that is 8 bits long would have no parity, and a unit of data 7 bits long would have an even parity bit to make an 8-bit word. Parity is used to check a unit of data for errors during transmission through phone lines or null modem cables.

Paste

To insert information from the clipboard. Information can be pasted multiple times.

Path

A route used in finding, retrieving and storing files on a disk. The course leading from the root directory of a drive to a particular file.

PDF

Portable document format. A PDF file is an electronic facsimile of a printed document.

Peer-to-peer

A network setup that allows every computer to both offer and access network resources, such as shared files, without requiring a centralised file server. Macintosh computers utilise this type of network setup.

Peripheral

A piece of hardware that's outside the main computer. It usually refers to external hardware such as disk drives, printers and scanners sold by a third party.

PERL

Practical extraction and reporting language. A robust programming language frequently used for creating CGI programs on web servers.

Pixel

Picture element. Digital images are composed of touching pixels, each having a specific colour or tone. The eye merges differently coloured pixels into continuous tones.

Pixel skipping

A means of reducing image resolution by simply deleting pixels throughout the image.

PKZIP/PKUNZIP

A software compression utility for the PC. It allows you to compress or 'zip' a file or a number of files into one archive file in the ZIP file format.

Plug-in

Extends the capabilities of a web browser, allowing the browser to run multimedia files.

Port

One of several rendezvous points where TCP/IP connections can be made on a computer. Ports are numbered, with several locations reserved for specific types of network activity, such as TELNET on port 23, HTTP traffic on port 80 and USENET news (NNTP) on port 119.

Posterisation

The conversion of continuous tone data into a series of visible tonal steps or bands.

ppi/ppc

Pixels per inch or pixels per centimetre. Units of measurement for scanned images.

PPP

Point-to-point protocol. It provides a method for transmitting packets over serial point-to-point links.

Primary colour

A base colour that is used to compose the other colours.

Process ink colours

CMYK pigments used in printing processes, chosen to produce the widest range of colour mixtures.

Profile

The colour characteristics of an input or output device, used by a CMS to ensure colour fidelity.

Properties

Information about an object, including settings or options for that object. For example, you look at properties of a file for information such as the file size, file type and file attributes.

Protocols

When data is being transmitted between two or more devices something needs to govern the controls that keep this data intact. A formal description of message formats and the rules two computers must follow to exchange those messages. Protocols can describe low-level details of machine-to-machine interfaces (*e.g., the order in which bits and bytes are sent across wire*) or high-level exchanges between application programs (*e.g., the way in which two programs transfer a file across the Internet*).

Proxy ARP

A technique in which one machine, usually a gateway, answers ARP requests for another machine. By pretending to be the physical network location of another machine, the gateway takes over the responsibility of routing packets destined for the other machine. For instance, a gateway can proxy ARP for addresses that the gateway identifies as being off the local network and that the gateway has a route for. The originating computer receives the gateway's proxy ARP reply and sends the datagram on to the gateway, which routes the datagram to its actual destination network.

PSN

Packet switch node; a store-and-forward packet switch (*formerly called an IMP*).

Public domain

Software that has no copyright or fee, which means you can copy, use, and even alter and sell it.

Quality factor

A multiplication factor (between 1 and 2) applied to output screen ruling to calculate scanning resolution for optimum output quality. This is also known as the halftoning factor.

Quarter tones

Tones between shadow and midtones are known as three-quarter tones and those between highlight and midtones are known as quarter tones.

Query

The process by which a web client requests specific information from a web server, based on a character string that is passed along.

QuickTime

A file extension for videos or 'movies' (like animations) compressed using their QuickTime format.

RAM

Random access memory. RAM is the most common type of computer memory, and it's where the computer stores system software, programs, and data you are currently using. It's formally called dynamic RAM (DRAM) because it's volatile, that is, the contents are lost when you turn off the computer (or crash). It's pronounced *ram* and measured in megabytes.

Raster

A synonym for grid. Sometimes used to refer to the grid of addressable positions in an output device.

Rel

Recorder element. The minimum distance between two recorded points (spots) in an imagesetter.

Remote system

Another computer on the Internet to which you connect. Interactions between computers are often described using the terms 'local' and 'remote' systems. The local system is your computer and the remote system is the other computer.

Res

A term used to define image resolution instead of ppi. Res 12 indicates 12 pixels per millimetre.

Resampling

An increase or reduction in the number of pixels in an image, required to change its resolution without altering its size. *See also* **down-sampling** and **interpolation**.

Resolution

In general, this refers to how sharp and clear an image looks on screen or on paper, and how much detail you can see. It's usually determined by the number of dots (or pixels) per square inch (the more there are, the higher the resolution) and is used to describe printers, monitors and scanners.

RGB

Red, green and blue are the primary colours of light perceived by the eye.

RIP

Routing information protocol used by Berkeley UNIX systems to exchange routing information among a set of computers attached to a network. RIP packets are sent and received by a program called routed.

ROM

Read-only memory. It's like software that's hard-wired into your computer – basic, permanent information that tells it things like how to load up the operating system when you turn it on.

Router

A special purpose computer that attaches to two or more networks and routes packets from one network to the other. A router uses network layer addresses (*such as IP addresses*) to determine if packets should be sent from one network to another. Routers send packets to other routers until they arrive at their final destination.

rpi

Rels (recorder elements) per inch. A measurement of the number of discrete steps that exposure units in imagesetting devices can make per inch.

RTF

Rich text format. A file format for text files that includes formatting instructions. Also called interchange format.

Sampling

The process of converting analogue data into digital data by taking a series of samples or readings at equal time intervals.

Saturation

The extent to which one or two of the three RGB primaries predominate in a colour. As quantities of RGB equalise, colour becomes desaturated towards grey or white.

Scanner

A device that converts images (such as photographs) into digital form so that they can be stored and manipulated on computers.

Screen frequency

The number of rows or lines of dots in a halftone image within a given distance, normally stated in lines per inch (lpi) or lines per centimetre (lpm). A frequency of 200 lpi would only be used in high-quality printing.

Screen ruling

Another term used for screen frequency.

Screen saver

A moving picture or pattern that is displayed on the screen when no activity takes place for a specified period of time.

Scripts

A type of program that consists of a set of instructions for another application or utility to use.

Scroll bar

The bar that appears at the right side or the bottom of a window that contains more information that can be displayed. The scroll bar is used to scroll an object or parts of a document into view when the entire object or document does not fit in the window.

Search engines

A type of software that creates indexes of databases or Internet sites based on the titles of files, key words, or the full text of files.

Second original

High-quality, contone reproduction of an image, intended to be identical to the original.

Secondary colour

Colour obtained by mixing two primary colours. Although known as primary colourants, C, M and Y are the secondary colours of light. Red plus green produce yellow, for example.

Serial cable/serial port

A cable used to connect peripheral devices through a computer's serial port. Normally a 25-pin connector on each end, yet can be a 9-pin on one. A **serial port** can either be plugged into an expansion slot on the motherboard of your computer or built into the motherboard itself. Serial ports are used for such devices as printers, mice and modems.

Server

A computer that shares its resources, such as printers and files, with other computers on the network. An example of this is a Novell NetWare Server which shares its disk space with a workstation that does not have a disk drive of its own.

Service (NT service)

A process that performs a specific function in Windows NT and can be called by various other programs. Windows NT provides tools to monitor and administer services.

Shadow

The darkest area of an image.

Shareware

Software that you can try before you buy. It's distributed through online services, BBSs and user groups. You're allowed to try it out and give copies to others, but if you want to keep using it, you must pay the registration fee.

Site

Organisation or facility where a host is located.

Site-license

Through negotiations with a vendor, a renewable fee has been paid to allow a fixed number of copies of copyrighted software at one site.

SLIP

Serial line internet protocol. A protocol used to run IP over serial lines, such as telephone circuits or RS-232 cables, interconnecting two systems.

SMTP

Simple mail transfer protocol. Internet standard protocol for transferring electronic mail messages from one computer to another. SMTP specifies how two mail systems interact and the format of control messages they exchange to transfer mail.

Socket

Logical address of a communications access point to a specific device or program on a host.

SPAM

Refers to the practise of blindly posting commercial messages or advertisements to a large number of unrelated and uninterested newsgroups.

Speckling

Isolated light pixels in predominantly dark image areas, sometimes caused by incorrect readings or noise in the scanning device.

Spectral highlight

A bright reflection from a light source containing little or no detail.

Spectrophotometer

An extremely accurate colour measurement device using a diffraction grating to split light into its components' wavelengths, which are then measured by numerous light sensors.

Spreadsheet

A number-related document whereby calculations and formulas are applied to the data organised in rows and columns of cells.

SQL

Structured query language. A syntax used by many database systems to retrieve and modify information.

Start/stop bits

A start bit signals the start of a unit of data in asynchronous communications. A stop bit signals the stop of a unit of data. The unit can vary in length depending on the protocol.

Substrate

The base material used to carry out or support an image, for example, paper or film.

Supersampling

The capture of more grey levels per colour than is required for image manipulation or output. This additional data allows shadow details to be heightened, for example.

Syntax error

Occurs when a user (or programmer) has put words in an order that a program does not understand.

Tags

Formatting codes used in HTML documents. These tags indicate how the parts of a document will appear when displayed by a web client program.

Taskbar

An area that runs across the bottom (usually) of the Windows desktop. Running applications are represented as buttons on the taskbar, the current window is shown as a depressed button, all other applications are displayed as raised buttons.

TCP

Transmission control protocol. This is a transport layer protocol that establishes a reliable, full duplex, data delivery service used by many TCP/IP application programs. The TCP software uses the IP protocol to transmit information across the Internet.

TCP/IP

Transmission control protocol/Internet protocol. A set of protocols, resulting from ARPA efforts, used by the Internet to support services such as remote login (TELNET), file transfer (FTP) and mail (SMTP).

Terminal

Communication device that lets a user send information to a computer by typing on a keyboard, and prints responses from the computer on paper or a screen.

Terminal mode

Many communications programs allow you to mimic a computer terminal, which is basically a keyboard and CRT display and/or a printer. A common terminal mode emulator is VT-100.

Terminal ready (TR)

This light is illuminated when your computer has turned on the RS-232 (serial) interface. Sometimes this light will not come on until you have loaded your communications software into memory.

Terminal server

A small, specialised, networked computer that connects many terminals to a LAN through one network connection. A terminal server can also connect network users to asynchronous ports or a host.

Threshold

The point at which an action begins or changes. The threshold setting used in scanning line art determines which pixels are converted to black and which will become white. The threshold defined in the USM process determines how large a tonal contrast must be before sharpening will be applied to it.

TIFF

Tag image file format. A graphic file format, TIFF files are also bit-maps, but they can be any size, resolution or colour depth. It is the most versatile, reliable and widely supported bit-mapped format and is the standard format for saving scanned images. However, the format does have several variations which means that occasionally an application may have trouble opening a TIFF file created by another program.

Title bar

The horizontal bar at the top of a window. The title bar shows the name of the window.

Toolbar

A collection of buttons that typically make the more common tools for an application easily accessible.

UNIX

An operating system developed by Bell Laboratories that supports multi-user and multi-tasking operations.

Upload

Send a file to another computer using a modem.

UPS

Uninterruptible power supply. A unit that switches to battery power whenever the power cuts out.

URI

Uniform resource identifier. A string of characters that represents the location or address of a resource on the Internet and how that resource should be accessed. A URI is a superset of the uniform resource locator.

URL

Uniform resource locator. A string of characters that represents the location or address of a resource on the Internet and how that resource should be accessed. World Wide Web pages are assigned a unique URL. Each hyperlink on a web page contains the URL of the page to be linked to.

USENET

A network of newsgroups. There are thousands of newsgroups available through USENET. Each one covers a specific topic or subject area.

User id

The string of characters that identifies you. The name by which you are known to the network. Also known as username.

UUCP

UNIX-to-UNIX copy program. This was initially a program run under the UNIX operating system that allowed one UNIX system to send files to another UNIX system via dial-up phone lines. Today, the term is more commonly used to describe the large international network which uses the UUCP protocol to pass news and electronic mail.

Virus

A program that replicates itself from one file or disk to another without your consent. They are spread through floppy disks, networks and online services and can go undetected (unless you have an antiviral utility) until something goes wrong. Some viruses deliberately destroy data, and even those designed to be *benign* can cause crashes, slowdowns and file corruption.

VRAM

Video RAM. A type of memory dedicated to handling the image displayed on a monitor. VRAM is built into many Macs, and it also comes on display cards.

Wallpaper

A graphical pattern displayed on the desktop.

Web browser

Also known as a web client program, this software allows you to access and view HTML documents. Internet Explorer, Netscape, Mosaic, Lynx, WinWeb and MacWeb are some examples of web browsers.

Web page

A document created with HTML that is part of a group of hypertext documents or resources available on the World Wide Web.

Webmaster

A person or group of people who maintain and administer a web server. Webmaster also refers to a standard e-mail address at most web hosts where comments and questions can be sent.

White point

A movable reference point that defines the lightest area in an image, causing all other areas to be adjusted accordingly.

WHOIS

An Internet program which allows users to query databases of people and other Internet entities, such as domains, networks and hosts. The information for people generally shows a person's company name, address, phone number and e-mail address.

Wide area network (WAN)

Network spanning multiple geographic distances, usually connected by telephone lines, microwave, or satellite links.

Wildcard

A character (usually * or ?) that can stand for one or more unknown characters during a search.

Word processing

Entering, editing and formatting text with the use of spelling checkers, outlining, tables, footnotes, and tables of contents.

Workstation

A networked personal computing device with more power than a standard IBM PC or Macintosh. Typically, a workstation has an operating system such as UNIX that is capable of running several tasks at the same time. It has several megabytes of memory and a large high-resolution display.

WWW

World Wide Web or W3 is the hypermedia document presentation system that can be accessed over the Internet using software called a web browser.

WYSIWYG

What you see is what you get. The image you see on the screen matches what will print on paper. Pronounced *wizzy-wig*.

Zipped

Compressed version of a program or document.

Index